ELUSIVE ISRAEL

ELUSIVE ISRAEL

The Puzzle of Election in Romans

Charles H. Cosgrove

Westminster John Knox Press
Louisville, Kentucky

© 1997 Charles H. Cosgrove

Unless otherwise indicated, all English translations of the Bible
are from the New Revised Standard Version of the Bible (NRSV),
copyright 1989 by the Division of Christian Education of the
National Council of the Churches of Christ in the U.S.A.,
and are used by permission.

All translations of Jewish pseudepigrapha are from *The Old Testament Pseudepigrapha*, ed.
James H. Charlesworth, 2 vols. (Garden City, N.Y.: Doubleday & Co., 1983, 1985).

Book design by Jennifer K. Cox
Cover design by Kevin Darst

First edition
Published by Westminster John Knox Press
Louisville, Kentucky

This book is printed on acid-free paper that meets the
American National Standards Institute Z39.48 standard. ♾

PRINTED IN THE UNITED STATES OF AMERICA
97 98 99 00 01 02 03 04 05 06 — 10 9 8 7 6 5 4 3 2 1

Library of Congress Cataloging-in-Publication Data

Cosgrove, Charles H.
    Elusive Israel : the puzzle of election in Romans / Charles H. Cosgrove. — 1st ed.
        p.   cm.
    Includes bibliographical references and index.
    ISBN 0-664-25696-1 (alk. paper)
    1. Bible. N.T. Romans—Criticism, interpretation, etc. 2. Paul, the Apostle,
Saint—Views on Israel (Christian theology) 3. Bible. N.T. Romans—Criticism,
Canonical. 4. Israel (Christian theology)—Biblical teaching. I. Title.
BS2545.I75C67   1997
227'.106—dc21

97-2542

To Katherine Grace

Contents

Acknowledgments

I would like to acknowledge a special debt to some friends who read portions of this book in draft and helped me to think better and write more clearly: Sherri C. Smith, a graduate student in the Department of English at Indiana University, and Lawrence Mattera and Raymond Mattera, two of my students. I also thank Rev. David Scott Smith for helping me prepare the notes and bibliography.

Portions of my article "The Church *with and for* Israel: History of a Theological *Novum* before and after Barth," *Perspectives in Religious Studies* 22 (1995): 259–78, have been included with permission.

Substantial parts of my article "Rhetorical Suspense in Romans 9—11: A Study in Polyvalence and Hermeneutical Election," *Journal of Biblical Literature* 115, 2 (1996): 271–87, have been reprinted in slightly modified form, with permission.

I dedicate this book to my daughter Katherine.

Introduction

What ought Christians do when faced with conflicting reasonable interpretations of scripture? That hermeneutical question drives this study of the identity and destiny of Israel in Romans.

At the dawn of the historical-grammatical (philological) approach to biblical interpretation, there was optimism that adherence to the plain grammatical sense could deliver interpretation from interminable debate over the true meaning of the text. The true meaning was taken to be the literal grammatical meaning, something a philological approach could be expected to ascertain. This optimism pervaded the Reformation period. Nevertheless, Protestant interpreters soon discovered that the grammatical sense was often unclear. Hence methods for negotiating historical-grammatical impasses in exegesis developed, notably the *analogia fidei* (interpreting according to the rule of faith) and the *analogia scripturae* (interpreting obscure passages of scripture in the light of "clear" ones). With the rise of self-consciously historical biblical theology in the late eighteenth century,[1] a renewed optimism arose that the sound and honest exegesis could provide clarity and certainty about obscure texts. That optimism would persist into the twentieth century, long after the warrants for such confidence had disappeared. One assumed that the true meaning of the text was the meaning originally intended by the author, and that this was the only valid meaning of the text as the church's scripture. Hence each new effort to clarify the original historical meaning of a difficult passage involved an at least implicit claim to represent the one, correct meaning of the text for the church. This was more attitude than theory, because no one worked out what the church was to do with equally plausible but conflicting interpretations by interpreters claiming to represent that original sense.

With the application in the nineteenth century of thoroughgoing historical-critical approaches to the Bible, the focus shifted to problems of reconstructing the history and ideas behind the text. But the older attitude remained. Historical-critical exegesis entailed the assumption that the real meaning of texts lies in the minds of their authors, and it conceived these authors as actors on the stage of history who had left behind texts as witnesses to their thought. In using the Bible as scripture, the church was to use the results of critical scholarship. This meant that the validity of any theological argument based on scripture depended on whether the argument used the correct (historically demonstrated) meaning of the scripture text(s) in question. But competing historical demonstrations of that meaning always existed. The individual biblical scholar committed to serving the church was therefore socialized into the practice of seeking to prove that his or her interpretation was the one, correct (most probable) interpretation, to the exclusion of all competitors. The nonscholar practitioner who made the effort to read more than one critical commentary found no guidance in the commentaries or in works of theological hermeneutics about what to do with more than one equally plausible historical interpretation. Trained theologians tended to adopt the hermeneutical attitude implicit in historical-critical exegesis as a discipline. Where theologians sought to adduce the sound exegesis on which their uses of scripture were based, they would invariably assert that this or that biblical scholar had "shown" that a biblical author meant such and such. But rarely had any such showing actually been made to the reasonable exclusion of all other interpretations. The emperor of assured exegetical results was often naked. But who could admit that, in making an argument that was supposed to depend on such results?

This is not to deny that we have made progress in our historical understanding of the Bible. There have, in fact, been enormous advances, especially over the last 150 years. But those advances include not only historical clarification of what the various biblical writings (and traditions) originally meant but also mounting evidence that many questions of exegesis cannot be historically resolved, because the texts themselves are irreducibly ambiguous. This is a momentous learning, and one that is just beginning to receive the attention it deserves.

The present study explores this learning in a very focused way, by examining how Paul's letter to the Romans structures "Israel" as an ambiguous sign in its smaller and larger arguments. I seek to show that we will never know with sufficient probability what the historical Paul's communicational intent was, to explain why this is so, and to demonstrate that we can nevertheless establish the limited range of interpretations that Paul's text warrants.

The shape of that range depends in part on *which* Romans we have in view—the historical Romans, as a document of early Christianity, or the canonical Romans, as a book of the Christian Bible.[2] My ultimate focus is the canonical Romans—a Romans that must be understood according to its original, historical meaning as that meaning is modified through the incorporation of the letter into the larger semantic context of the Christian Bible.

A further thesis of this study is that, unlike historical interpretation, canonical interpretation requires by its very nature a hermeneutic of use and therefore a method of adjudicating between competing plausible interpretations. In making such interpretive decisions, Christians ought to consider the larger canonical context, including the purpose of scripture. I propose that scripture's purpose is laid down by the canonical Jesus in Matt. 22:37–40. The implication of this passage is that interpretive judgments should be guided by the command "You shall love your neighbor as yourself." I seek to adjudicate the identity of Israel in Romans with this rule of interpretation in mind.

Chapter 1 explores the elusive identity of Israel in Romans by constructing an imaginary dialogue among three ancient Roman Christians shortly after the death of Paul. The annotations to this dialogue, together with a concluding analysis, demonstrate why the identity of true Israel is irreducibly indeterminate in Romans.

Chapter 2 examines Paul's uses of the ancient rhetorical device of co-deliberation with one's audience (*communicatio*). By virtue of the unresolvable ambiguity of certain features of Paul's argument in Romans 9–11, co-deliberation becomes a trope of our own hermeneutical situation: Paul invites us to choose what his text will mean within the limits of plausible exegesis. This leads to a discussion of the role of the "will" and the hermeneutical function of the purpose of scripture in canonical interpretation.

Chapter 3 considers how the incorporation of Romans into the Christian Bible affects the meaning of Paul's letter. Among the resultant "canonical effects" is what I term the conversion of *apocalyptic Paul* into *prophetic Paul.* The canon rewrites Pauline apocalyptic as contingent or provisional prophecy, rendering Paul one more in a long line of biblical prophets whose oracles do not limit God's freedom to act in surprising ways. Thus, Paul's oracle of the imminent salvation of "all Israel" and his teaching that the church exists already within the beginning of the End stands within a larger canonical story that assumes the continuance of history beyond the age of the apostles and thus implies that the divine revelation to Paul is not to be fulfilled in the way he expected.

Chapter 4 draws together the threads of the preceding chapters by adjudicating the question of Israel in the canonical Romans. Guided by the interpretive norm of the humane purpose of scripture, I take Paul to affirm that the Jewish people are true and irrevocably elect Israel. I then go on to present some clarifications and implications designed to enhance further (and thus to warrant more securely) this interpretation. These fall under the following headings: literal Israel as symbol and metaphor; nationalism and national differentiation in Pauline perspective; and the politics of God according to Romans 11.

1

Elusive Israel

Is Paul a radical Jewish sectarian who redefines Israel "spiritually" as those from all nations who believe the gospel and live "in Christ"? Or is he a rabbi who affirms the ongoing election of ethnic Israel but holds that God has sent Jesus Christ as a special way of salvation for the gentiles?[1] Perhaps the truth about Paul lies in between these two extremes or combines them in some way. For convenience, I have put some labels to views on such questions in the history of the exegesis of Romans:

> *Ecclesial Israelism.* While the name Israel can still be used in a conventional sense of the Jewish people, true Israel since Christ's appearance is the church. This ecclesial Israel is composed of people from the nations, including the Jewish nation. But Jewish identity counts for no more than that of any other people in the creation of this new, international people because in Christ all ethnic identities are immaterial. To this new ecclesial Israel, and not to the Jewish nation, belong the scriptures, the promises made to the patriarchs, the eschatological fulfillment of the covenants, and the hope of the new creation.

> *National Israelism.* The Jewish people, defined by genealogy and the practice of the law, are Israel, and God remains self-bound in love and saving purpose toward them. National Israel does not cease to be true Israel even when it rejects the gospel message preached by Christians. While suffering a partial hardening toward the gospel, the Jewish nation retains the vocation and destiny of Israel as set forth in the scriptures.

> *Elect Remnant Israelism.* True Israel has always been composed of an elect, faithful few among the Jewish people. Now that the messiah has appeared, this elect Israel is the company of Jews who have believed the gospel message. Thus they

constitute an eschatological remnant within the Jewish nation. As elect Israel, they also share an identity as God's people with the elect of the other nations, who possess the blessings of the gospel and are destined for eschatological glory.

Since the rise of the historical-critical method, considerable effort has
been devoted to discovering which of these positions, if any, the historical
Paul supported. But an equally important question—and for some purposes, a more important question—is which of these views, if any, Romans
best supports. By this I mean Romans the *text*, the meaning of which is at
least theoretically and may be, in significant respects, factually distin-
guishable from the historical Paul's intent.

The original, historical meaning of Romans the text is what the original audience of the text would have been justified in taking it to mean. This
follows from a commonsense rule of language use that we all regularly apply when, for example, we tell someone, "That may be what you meant,
but it's not what you said."[2] Thus a text's meaning may or may not coin-
cide with what the author was trying to communicate. It may say something other than what the author meant; it may say more than its author
had in mind; it may be ambiguous. Hence the author's *communicational* intent may differ from the *apparent* intent of that author in the text.

I therefore refer to textual meaning as *apparent intent.* By this I mean not
a reader's superficial impression of a text's intent but rather what emerges
as the "apparent meaning" after careful scrutiny and demonstration.[3] One
can also call this "public meaning," since it is the interpretation warranted
by common, public language use.

The apparent or public meaning of the historical Romans is determined
by the shared language of Paul and his audience—a shared cultural-
linguistic lexicon. This is the *semantic context* of the letter. The historical
Romans is further determined by the situation of Paul and his audience, a
situation conditioned by the history leading up to the writing of the letter
and thus by early church politics. This is the *rhetorical context.* Moreover,
Romans is part of the Christian Bible and therefore has a *canonical context*
as well. My focus in this chapter is Romans the text as situated beyond the
original rhetorical situation of Romans, at the point where the letter first
enters what Brevard Childs has called the "canonical process."[4] Hence I
look at Romans as a text that does not yet have a canonical context but that
is already being regarded as an authority in its own right—an authority independent of the living Paul, who at one time might have clarified or modified what he wrote in this letter.

In envisioning this Romans, I imagine how three hypothetical Roman
Christians could fairly have interpreted Romans after Paul's death, at a
time when the church had just decided to make readings from Romans part

of regular worship services. This moment in the history of Romans is conceptually significant because it helps us represent the historical Romans at a moment when it becomes an authoritative *text* for a congregation as a whole.[5] If, while Paul was still alive, the Roman Christians argued about the meaning of the letter because they needed to adopt a stance *toward* the living, individual Paul, henceforth they would argue about its meaning because they wished to argue *from* Paul's text. I hold this to be one fundamental sense in which the biblical writings serve as canon: they are texts that we Christians argue *from* as we seek to influence church decision making. While there are other ways in which the Bible functions as scripture, it is the use of the Bible as a basis of public appeal within the church that concerns me in this study.

Therefore we will imagine some hypothetical Roman Christians debating the meaning of Romans after the death of Paul.[6] These readers do not belong to the original rhetorical situation of the letter, but they do share the common lexicon of Paul and his original audience. Hence what they are warranted in arguing from Romans counts as a valid interpretation of the historical Romans.

⟨ ⟩

One last set of preliminary clarifications is in order before we proceed. In this and subsequent chapters, I use the term *nation* in a broad sense to mean a "people," which may or may not be a political entity. I also use the term *carnal* interchangeably with the words *ethnic* and *fleshly* to designate Israel as the Jewish people—Israel "according to the flesh" (cf. Rom. 9:5). While *carnal* and *fleshly* can have a pejorative sense, owing to their association in some streams of the Western Christian tradition with a negative view of the body, I do not subscribe to this attitude toward bodily existence and therefore do not use these terms with any pejorative connotations. But a discussion of this point will have to await chapter 4.

A Roman Dialogue

The readers I have in mind are a gentile Christian, whom I will call Chariton, and two Jewish Christians, whom I will name Simeon and Reuben.[7] Reuben and Chariton are great admirers of Paul and regard him as an inspired prophet and apostolic ambassador of Christ. They supported the decision that the church make it a practice to study Paul's letter and to read portions of it at community gatherings along with the Law and the Prophets. Simeon is one of a very few Jewish Christians who opposed this decision. He does not want Paul's letter to be read along with the scriptures because he strongly disagrees with what he takes to be Paul's views about the identity and destiny of the Jewish people.

The Jewish-Christian Reuben and the gentile Christian Chariton thus agree against Simeon. Nevertheless, Simeon and Reuben, who both continue to attend the synagogue, agree against Chariton that God's presence is still to be found in the synagogue, because God has promised never to forsake Israel. While Reuben believes that Paul's letter to the Roman church supports this theological position, Chariton and Simeon think that Paul opposes it. Simeon sees Paul as a Jewish apostate. He claims that it was Paul's custom to apply the name Israel to the churches he founded and that Paul regarded only Christians as the "true circumcision," whether or not they were circumcised in the flesh. Both Simeon and Chariton find this view reiterated in Romans. Reuben has a different understanding. According to him, Romans 11 confirms the teaching that all carnal Israel, the dispersed nation as a whole, is true Israel and has a share in the age to come. Simeon would like to believe this, but he, like Chariton, is convinced that Paul's letter contains no such affirmations about the Jewish people, much less allows for the view that God's Spirit is found in the synagogue.

All three know Paul's letter very well. All three also assume that what Paul teaches about Israel is internally consistent, and each one seeks, accordingly, to construct consistent interpretive arguments as restatements of Paul's argument. In their discussion, parts of which I present below, they have been thoughtful enough to speak in English and to refer to Romans according to its canonical versification. Since readers may find it difficult to keep the three characters straight according to their basic opinions and attitudes, I suggest that one associate the gentile name Chariton with a "charitable" attitude toward Paul, the Jewish name Simeon with a "suspicious" attitude toward Paul (whom Simeon regards as a radical "sectarian"), and the Jewish name Reuben with the "rabbinic" view that "all Israel has a share in the age to come"—a view that Reuben attributes to Paul. Only Simeon interprets Paul from a horizon of suspicion, but the interesting thing about the debate is that Chariton's hermeneutic of trust, rooted in a gentile bias, leads to the same interpretation of Romans as does Simeon's hermeneutic of suspicion.[8] Thus, Reuben, who is a champion of Paul, asserts an interpretation of Romans that both Simeon and Chariton reject.

When we begin to eavesdrop on their conversation, our three interlocutors are discussing the theme of divine impartiality in Paul. In judging the world, Paul says, God will show no favoritism toward Jew or gentile (2:6–11). According to Simeon and Chariton, Paul means that God pays no attention to whether someone is a Jew or a Greek. Reuben objects. He observes Paul's assertion that divine wrath and blessing will be meted out to "the Jew first" (2:9–10). By giving the Jew this priority in the judgment, Reuben argues, Paul is implicitly honoring the priority of the Jewish people as elect Israel, which shows that Paul affirms God's unbreakable covenant with the Jewish people.

SIMEON: But this priority expresses no covenantal advantage for Jews. To be treated first in the same way as the gentiles! Paul is being ironic when he says, "To the Jew first." He is mocking the election of Israel.

REUBEN: You don't need to take it that way. Paul is only saying that God will judge the world by the standards of righteousness revealed to us in the law. We Jews have an advantage in possessing the law, just as Paul says: we have been "entrusted with the oracles of God" (3:2). And when he says, "To the Jew first," three times in the first part of the letter, twice in a positive sense, that is his way of assuring his readers that he is not contesting the election of Israel.

SIMEON: How can the election of Israel stand if God treats Jews and gentiles in the same way, as if there were no difference? Which is exactly what Paul goes on to say: "There is no distinction between Jew and Greek" (10:12). The impartiality of God is one thing. To say that it means there is no distinction between Jew and gentile is something else. It is to deny God's covenant with Israel.

In an extensive survey of Jewish uses of the principle of divine impartiality, Jouette Bassler has found no Jewish writing (besides Romans and a difficult-to-date rabbinic midrash) in which this axiom provides a basis for arguing that God makes no distinction between Jews and gentiles.[9] In view of this, it makes sense for Simeon to contend that Paul's use of the axiom of divine impartiality contradicts God's promises to Israel.[10] To Reuben, however, closer examination shows that in Paul's view, God is impartial and also faithful to his promises.

REUBEN: I agree that in this part of the letter Paul is provoking Israel, but he is only goading the Jewish people the way Jewish prophets have always done. Hosea was much bolder when he announced that God had divorced Israel.

SIMEON: True, but Hosea also preached that God remarried Israel, not that God took a new wife and called her Israel.

REUBEN: You put the worst construction on Paul.

CHARITON: On the contrary! It was revealed to Paul that the true people of God in these last days are those who accept the gospel. The true Israelites are those who are led by the Spirit of Christ. The rest of the Jews and the gentiles stand under God's wrath.

Reuben might respond by pointing out that even if this were Paul's view, it would not necessarily mean that fleshly Israel's election has been canceled, unless Paul were claiming that God's verdict against fleshly Israel is final. As long as God keeps making a new start for Israel, as God has always done, God's honor is not compromised. Therefore, if Paul affirms that the election of Israel endures even through divine judgment, then Paul has not impugned God's trustworthiness. But Reuben is also bothered by Chariton's insinuation that Torah-faithful Jews who have not believed in Jesus stand under God's wrath, as if their obedience to the law did not count with God.

REUBEN: Again you overstate Paul's views. For one thing, he says that there are gentiles who do not possess the law but do instinctively what the law requires. Some of them, he says, will receive God's approbation for their good works. These gentiles are neither God-fearers nor Christians, since God-fearers know the law and Christian gentiles fulfill the law not "instinctively" (φύσει: "by nature"), as 2:14 phrases it, but by the Spirit (see 8:1–4). So Paul is thinking about gentiles outside the synagogue and the church, whose moral life will win God's approval in the judgment. Surely, if Paul can imagine gentiles living righteously apart from Christ, he must allow that there are some Jews, perhaps many, who possess a righteousness pleasing to God even though they have not yet believed the gospel. God will reward them, too, in the final judgment.

The gentiles that Reuben has in mind are the sort that Jews admired— gentiles who practiced what many diaspora Jews thought of as the "common ethic," to use John J. Collins's apt phrase.[11] They are Torah-faithful people who have been hardened in God's providence so that they refuse the gospel (11:25) but otherwise do live righteous lives according to the law, which would naturally have included confessing their sins and seeking God's forgiveness according to the law's own provisions for sin.[12] In many ways they *are* guides to the blind, lights to those in darkness, correctors of the foolish (see 2:19–20). The name of God is not blasphemed among the gentiles because of *them* (2:24). On the contrary, they are the sorts of Jews whom many gentiles admired.[13]

CHARITON: You put too much weight on a possibility that Paul only says "might" be the case with some gentiles. And you miss the irony. When God judges the world according to deeds, there may be a few Jews and there may be a few gentiles whose good lives win God's approval. But the point is that even in rewarding a few righteous Jews, God shows no partiality to Israel. These few are rewarded by God just like their gentile counterparts; and the many Jews will receive "wrath and fury" just like their gentile counterparts. For Jews and gentiles are alike "under sin" (3:9).

REUBEN: Whether many or few will receive any praise from God, Paul does not say. But you make the mistake of assuming that if only a few are rewarded for their works, then Paul is denying the election of Israel. As if God could not be forgiving toward Israel! I think you must put Paul's teaching about judgment according to works together with his teaching about God's mercy. Do not our rabbis teach that God may show mercy to Israel for the sake of the righteous ones? When Moses pleads with God on behalf of Israel, is his prayer not heard? And will not God be merciful to us for the sake of his own righteousness, according to his promises? "Although everyone is a liar, let God be proved true" (3:4).

When the rabbis considered the sins of Israel as a whole, they also imagined God finding merciful ways to be just, such as saving the many for the sake of the righteous few or for the sake of God's own righteousness.[14]

SIMEON: Paul mentions no divine mercy toward anyone until he speaks of the righteousness of God revealed in Christ. Now that the Christ has come, God's mercy is found in Christ. But God's merciful righteousness helps only those who believe the gospel (3:21–26). You see how he shuts Israel out, treating us just like the gentiles. But you imagine that Paul affirms God's unbreakable covenant with our people and that he expects God to be merciful to the whole nation of Israel in fulfillment of the covenant. So either you make Paul contradict himself or you really do not believe him when he says that God treats all nations alike.

REUBEN: You fail to consider that God has always disciplined us Israelites for our sins. From generation to generation God has been a father to us, applying his chastening rod when we forsake his ways. By his merciful hand of judgment and by the sufferings of the righteous, God has prevented our sins from mounting up to heaven. With the gentiles it is otherwise. They need a special divine work to deal with the long record of their sins and to liberate them from their enslavement to their passions. That is why God has sent the Christ apart from the law, not to shut Israel out but to save the gentiles.[15]

In Paul's day, it was the conviction of at least some Jews that God judges and rewards the nation of Israel, as well as individual Israelites, according to a mercy not shown to the gentiles. According to this view, Jews would receive mercy in the eschatological judgment, while the rest of the world would suffer strict justice according to deeds. The *Psalms of Solomon* say that God will "repay sinners forever according to their actions" and "have mercy on the righteous" (2:34–35; cf. 15:10–13). The distinction between "the sinners" and "the righteous" expresses the sharp differentiation made in the *Psalms* between the lawless gentiles and Israel (cf. Paul's similar language in Gal. 2:15). By contrast, where the *Psalms* speak of Israel's sin, they teach that divine punishment for the nation's disobedience is a disciplining love aimed at correction and restoration (7 and 18). Thus, in *Pss. Sol.* 17:10, God's "faithfulness in judgment" is instanced by God's destruction of Israel's enemies, who have finished serving as the instrument of divine punishment against Jerusalem. A similar view of the purpose of divine judgment toward Israel is found in the *Testaments of the Twelve Patriarchs.* The *Testament of Naphtali*, for example, describes the Diaspora as a judgment on the nation that will come to an end when "the mercy of the Lord comes, a man who effects righteousness, and he will work mercy on all who are far and near" (*T. Naph.* 4:5; cf. *T. Iss.* 6:4; *T. Judah* 23:5). Other examples are found in *Jubilees* 1:5–18 and *2 Baruch* 13.

Moreover, in the *Psalms of Solomon*, the pattern of divine disciplining love is applied not only to the nation but to the righteous as individuals (13:7–12). The righteous, then, are not sinners like the gentiles. Not only are they committed to God's law, they are also God's children. When they sin, they can count on God's mercy. And even if they should confess that "no one living is righteous before you [God]," as the biblical psalmist does (Ps. 143:2; cf. Rom. 3:20), they can nonetheless trust that they will be rewarded for their good works within a framework of divine mercy. Thus, Sirach says that those who "fear the Lord" and "keep his ways" know that they shall "fall into the hands of the Lord, and not into the hands of human beings; for as his greatness is, so is his mercy" (Sir. 2:15–18; my translation). According to the Similitudes of *1 Enoch*, the judgment of the elect by the Lord of the Spirits is "according to his mercy and his patience" (60:25; cf. 61:13). In the *Apocalypse of Zephaniah*, the seer, who is clearly numbered among the righteous, prays that God will erase the manuscript of his sin, "because your mercy has [co]me to be in every place and has filled every [pl]ace" (7:8). And even the pessimistic *4 Ezra* expresses the hope that the God who judges the nations and Israel with severity will save a remnant of Israel through mercy (12:34). To be sure, the idea of the remnant is radically qualifying here. But the classical rabbinic view expressed in *Sanhedrin* 10:1 appears to have been generally affirmed within nonsectarian strands of Second Temple Judaism: "All Israel has a share in the world to come" (cf. *T. Benj.* 10:11). While apostates would have been excluded, the majority of Jews were included: "Not only the righteous, but also the vast majority of Israelites—neither completely righteous nor utterly wicked—have a share in the world to come."[16]

REUBEN: I don't make Paul contradict himself. Paul says that "God imprisoned all in disobedience so that he may be merciful to all." This is part of the mystery in which Paul discloses the salvation of all Israel (11:25–26). If God saves all Israel because of his righteousness and because of the patriarchs, then he is showing mercy to those shut up under disobedience (11:28–32). As for the other nations, do not the words "Be merciful to all" (11:32) mean that God's mercy toward the nations will be in equal measure to his mercy toward Israel? Are not the nations also beloved, for the sake of Abraham, who is the father of all the nations, just as Israel is beloved for the sake of the fathers? Paul asks the gentiles to ruminate about the fate of Israel and to imagine a restoration of the nation as a whole (11:11ff.). I think that we Christian Jews should likewise ruminate about the fate of the nations and entertain the possibility that in the end, God will show mercy to all people and not just to the few Jews and gentiles who have accepted the gospel.[17]

CHARITON: But there is another more natural way to interpret Paul without making him contradict himself. "All Israel" does not refer to Israel according to the flesh, for not all from fleshly Israel are true Israel (9:6). True Israel is made up of true Jews. Some true Jews are found among the uncircumcised, those gentile Christians who keep the requirements of the law from the heart by the power of the Spirit (2:26–29 and 8:1–4). Others are Jewish Christians, who shall eventually make up the full number of elect from among the circumcised, the "fullness" (πλήρωμα) spoken of in 11:12.

SIMEON: Yes, I agree. Paul is one of those fanatical seers who say that the nation will perish but the elect will be saved.

CHARITON: Then there is what Paul calls the "fullness" (πλήρωμα) of the gentiles. When this elect number of gentiles has been gathered in, all Israel—*true* Israel—will be saved. There will be no special provision for the Jewish nation. All the nations, including the Jewish nation, will perish, but the elect will be saved, for God shows no partiality.

Chariton takes Paul's statement "Not all Israelites truly belong to Israel" (9:6b) in a sectarian sense. Only the elect *within* ethnic Israel belong to Israel, which now includes both Jews and gentiles (9:24). Thus he finds in 9:6–29 a description of a line of election that is not based on conventional notions of Jewish identity. In the present time, this line issues in a true Israel made up of Jews and gentiles: the remnant. This true Israel corresponds to the true Jews, as defined in 2:25–29.

Interpreters today are divided on the question of how Paul defines Israel in 9:6ff.[18] According to a traditional view, which continues to find strong defenders,[19] Paul is defining true Israel in the present time as the church. But a growing number of scholars now argue that in 9:6ff. he uses

the example of God's methods in electing Israel only to defend the claim
that God is free to constitute, in the present time, a new people of promise
made up of both Jews and gentiles.

Advocates of the first interpretation think that, in chapter 9, Paul is redefining Israel all the way through v. 29, with the result that "Israel" from that
point on in the letter can be used in either of the two senses suggested by
v. 6b ("Not all who are descended from Israel belong to Israel"; RSV): there is
Israel according to the flesh and Israel according to election. With the advent
of the messiah, true Israel, which once existed exclusively within ethnic Israel,
overlaps with ethnic Israel. Likewise, the remnant, as true Israel, is no longer
found exclusively within ethnic Israel; it merely overlaps with fleshly Israel.

According to advocates of the second interpretation,[20] the explication of
the thesis stated in 9:6b ("Not all who are descended from Israel belong to
Israel"; RSV) is completed in vv. 6–13. Jews in Paul's time did, of course,
use the expressions "Israel" and "children of Abraham" interchangeably,
but in fact, not all of Abraham's children are Israelites. Ishmael and Esau
are descendants of Abraham but stand outside the line of promise. In this
sense, then, "not all from Israel are Israel." Paul's point is that, although
God made the promises to Abraham and his descendants, scripture records
that God used elective freedom in establishing, within Abraham's poster-
ity, the line of heirs called Israel (from Jacob onward). In a later stage of his
argument (vv. 14–29), Paul appeals to this same elective freedom to argue
that God is now creating a new people of promise—not to displace Israel
or establish a "new" Israel but to include the gentiles.

There are also variations of these two interpretations, including some
that seem to combine elements of both. James Dunn, for example, rejects
the interpretation that equates true Israel with the church, and he interprets
"all Israel" in 11:26 to mean Paul's Jewish kinfolk as a whole.[21] Yet he argues that Paul does mean to include the gentiles mentioned in 11:25 within
Israel.[22] This suggests that Paul uses the name Israel in more than one way.
Some maintain that Paul defines Israel in contradictory ways. According to
J. Christiaan Beker, for example, Paul identifies true Israel with the church,
later with the Jewish remnant, and finally with the whole Jewish people.[23]

Chariton construes Rom. 2:25–29 and Rom. 9:6–29 in mutually reinforcing ways and opts for a compatible interpretation of 11:25ff. According to Rom. 2:26, uncircumcised people who keep the precepts of the law
are regarded by God as circumcised. Chariton thinks Paul is now talking
about Christian gentiles, since Paul says that this true circumcision is
"spiritual" (ἐν πνεύματι, 2:29; cf. the significant parallel in 8:1–4). Some
modern commentators understand the text in this way as well.[24]

Chariton is correct in observing that Paul uses the same word to designate both the "fullness" of the gentiles (11:25) and the "fullness" of his kinfolk (11:12). Chariton concludes from this that just as an elect number of

gentiles will be saved, so *only* an elect number within fleshly Israel will be saved.[25] This interpretation is also consistent with Paul's statement that he magnifies his ministry to the gentiles in order to make his kinspeople jealous and thus save "some" of them (11:14). The idea of an elect number of Israelites is found in the writings of Jewish separatists. The sectarian idea of a remnant—a remnant of true Israel distinguished *from* but *not for the sake of* Israel as a whole—appears to be operative in the *Community Rule* at Qumran.[26] This contrasts with the concept of the remnant as a means of hope for Israel as a whole and ultimately, in the rabbinic conception, as a sign of God's pledge that all Israel has a share in the age to come (see above).

REUBEN: When Paul speaks of spiritual circumcision, he may be referring to the work of God's Spirit in Christ, but he could be referring to the work of God's Spirit before the appearance of Christ—the activity of God's Spirit in generations of Israelites committed from the heart to God.[27] In any case, Paul is talking about the meaning of circumcision as a sign of righteousness. His point is that circumcision is not a mark of righteousness unless one keeps the law. It follows that if gentiles turn to God in obedience to the gospel of God's messiah, and if they keep the law from the heart and by the Spirit, then they have the circumcised hearts of which Jeremiah spoke. This does not mean that fleshly circumcision is no longer a sign of membership in the covenant people of Israel. Paul teaches both the literal meaning of circumcision, as a sign of election, and the spiritual meaning of circumcision, as a sign of righteousness. Gentiles can share in the spiritual meaning. Jews are called to be faithful to both the literal and the spiritual.

SIMEON: But Paul says that the children of Abraham are those who share the faith that Abraham had before he was circumcised, that is, when he was a gentile. The circumcised become heirs of Abraham only by sharing this gentile form of faith, apart from circumcision and the law. According to Paul, our circumcision does not count one way or another in qualifying us as Abraham's children. And if we are "adherents of the law," then we are in a place of wrath (4:14–15)! Doesn't that mean that the only way for Jews to escape God's wrath is to abandon the law and become gentiles?[28]

REUBEN: The whole world is liable to God's wrath, including Israel. Being a son of the law does not exempt anyone from God's impartial judgment—a judgment that the law itself delivers against Israelites when they sin (3:9–20). But Paul does not deny that the Jewish people are God's elect people Israel. He himself says explicitly, "They are Israelites, and to them belong the adoption, the glory, the covenants. . . . " Most of them are hardened toward the gospel, but even that is in the providence of God. It is God's way of making room for the gentiles (11:19–20). Yet because they are Israelites, God will save them after the fullness of the gentiles comes in (11:25–26). Perhaps, for the time being, most of the circumcised children of Abraham are liable to God's wrath, even though they are Israelites destined for salvation. But those like us, who already share the faith of Abraham by believing the gospel, are now living in the sphere of God's kindness. The same applies to the gentiles who share Abraham's faith. That is all Paul means.

SIMEON: But Paul implies that circumcision is *not* a sign that we Jews are the heirs of Abraham. So there is no escaping the inference that the only way for Jews to become the true descendants of Abraham is for them to abandon the law and become gentiles like Abraham.

REUBEN: You keep failing to see that circumcision has a double meaning in Paul's letter. There is the circumcision of the flesh, which is a sign of God's irrevocable pledge to Israel. Then there is the spiritual meaning of circumcision, as a sign of faith and of obedience from the heart. The circumcision of Abraham signifies both faith *and* the election of the circumcised. But because the circumcised are under the power of sin just like the other nations, God confirms the *election* of Israel through the faith of Abraham, in which gentiles can share as well.

CHARITON: I do not find any place in Romans where Paul says that fleshly circumcision is a sign of the election of Israel according to the flesh. Paul says that circumcision is of value if you keep the law; circumcision is a sign of being entrusted with the oracles of God; and Abraham's circumcision is a sign of his faith, meaning that the gentiles who share his faith are also his heirs. But notice that he does not say, "If it is *only* the adherents of the law who are to be the heirs, then faith is null and the promise is void" (see 4:14). That is what *you* wrongly attribute to him. But what Paul says in 4:14 means that if faith and the promise are to stand, then those from the law are *not* heirs.

SIMEON: Exactly. According to Paul, we Jews become heirs of Abraham only by becoming gentiles in faith. Nothing else counts: not being from the law, not fleshly circumcision, not being the fleshly descendants of Abraham.

REUBEN: I understand why you construe Paul's midrash on Abraham the way you do. Once again, you imagine that he is trying to exclude Israel when he is only arguing for the inclusion of the gentiles. You read v. 14 too strictly and ignore v. 16, where Paul says that the promise is confirmed not only to adherents of the law but also to those who share the faith of Abraham.

CHARITON: No, Paul has already made it clear in 4:12 that the guarantee is restricted by the qualification of faith. Abraham is the father of the circumcised for those who are not only circumcised but also share his faith, which now means faith in Jesus.

REUBEN: You should rather say "faith in the one who raised Jesus from the dead" (cf. 4:24).

SIMEON: Which in the present time means faith in Jesus.

REUBEN: You should not so easily discount the faith of those who believe in the God of Abraham, who raises the dead. There are many who have this faith, although they have been given a partial blindness to the gospel by this same God.

CHARITON: Paul says that Abraham is the father of the circumcised who share his faith and of the uncircumcised who share his faith, nothing more—certainly nothing that allows for an irrevocable election of those from the law. You only think otherwise because you insist on making everything Paul says about the Jewish people fit your interpretation of that enigmatic passage in chapter 11 about the salvation of all Israel. Instead, you should pay attention to the basic point made over and over in the first part of the letter. There is no distinction between Jews and gentiles. In their inward selves, Jews and gentiles alike know what God requires of them. Some heed God from the heart, others do not. All will be judged on the basis of whether or not they do what is right. It makes no difference to God whether they are Jews or gentiles. And now that the messiah has been revealed, what God requires is that they obey the gospel. Those who obey shall be saved; the rest stand under God's wrath. It doesn't matter whether they are Jews or gentiles in any fleshly sense. Those who obey the gospel receive the Spirit and are circumcised in a true sense. In the eyes of God, who sees into the secret places of the heart and pays no attention to the flesh, the Christian churches are the real Jews and the real Israel.

SIMEON: Exactly. Which is why Paul feels obliged to answer the questions "Then what advantage does the Jew have?" and "What is the value of circumcision?"

Our three discussants next turn to Rom. 3:1–8. As Reuben sees it, the basic question addressed in these verses is whether God will remain faithful to his covenant promises to Israel. In Reuben's view, Paul's answer anticipates what he will say in chapters 9–11.[29] Rereading 3:1–8 in the light of chapter 11, Reuben "knows" that God's faithfulness (3:3), righteousness (3:5), and truth (3:7 cf. v. 4) mean, for Paul, that God will honor the promises to the Jewish people.[30] But Chariton objects to this approach. He insists that one ought to take 3:1–8 more strictly in terms of its immediate context, by construing the passage as a judgment text in which Paul explains why the advantage of being a Jew does not put Jews in a better position than gentiles when it comes to the outpouring of divine wrath. According to Chariton, the passage makes perfect sense if one understands God's faithfulness, truth, and righteousness to mean that God's honor is in no way impugned if God brings down wrath on unfaithful Jews. To be a righteous judge of the world, God must treat the Jews no differently than the gentiles. Chariton finds further confirmation of his interpretation in 3:9–20, where he sees no hint that God will be mercifully faithful to Jews because they are God's chosen people. Moreover, when Paul does speak about God's mercy, he stresses that it is toward Jew and gentile alike (3:21–31).

In response, Reuben reiterates his view that 3:1–8 affirms God's faithful mercy toward unfaithful Israel. This does not mean that God shows favoritism toward the Jews. God will be equally merciful toward the gentiles. According to 5:12–21, Christ's act of righteousness is more powerful than Adam's act of disobedience, which led to death for all. Therefore, the scope of Christ's achievement must be as wide as the consequences of the first man's sin: acquittal and life for all, not just a few. Likewise, in 11:32, Paul affirms that God's faithful mercy toward the nation of Israel will be matched by God's faithful mercy toward all the nations, to whom God is pledged by his promise to Abraham. Thus, Reuben agrees that the advantage of being a Jew and the value of circumcision do not put Jews in a superior position in relation to gentiles when it comes to God's merciful judgment.

CHARITON: So you are saying that the Jewish advantage is preserved because no sin by the nation of Israel can nullify God's faithfulness toward Israel? But why do you assume that one of the Jewish advantages is that God will remain forgiving toward Israel no matter what, that there is always divine mercy beyond judgment? Look at how Paul's argument unfolds in 3:1–8. God's faithfulness is vindicated in God's judgments, as the psalmist says, and Jews have no business suggesting that it would be unjust of God to inflict wrath on them. If God did not have the right to inflict wrath on the unrighteous, including Jews, how could God be the impartial judge of the world?

REUBEN: I agree with you—to a point. According to Paul, God has the right to inflict wrath on the Jewish people. That wrath is already being revealed (1:18ff.) toward the whole of humanity, and we Jews, like Paul, recognize that when God brings judgment on us, he is always in the right. Nevertheless, God remains faithful to us beyond judgment. You equate God's faithfulness and God's righteousness in judgment, as if God's faithfulness means faithfulness to himself—to his own standards of righteousness—and not faithfulness to the promises he has made to Israel. And you forget that God cannot be faithful to himself unless he honors his promises to Israel. This is why God's faithfulness is an advantage for the Jewish people. By affirming God's faithfulness and trustworthiness against Jewish unfaithfulness (3:3–4), Paul is asserting that God will be merciful to Israel beyond the divine rights of judgment and beyond the righteous wrath of which Paul goes on to speak. And this way of taking 3:3–4 is supported by Romans 11:26–29. All Israel will be saved because "the gifts and the calling of God are irrevocable."

CHARITON: And how will they be saved, unless they believe in Jesus Christ?

REUBEN: After the fullness of the gentiles comes in, God will remove the hardening that has come upon Israel, and they will recognize Jesus as the messiah.

CHARITON: Then you agree that as long as they persist in unbelief, God is not being unfaithful toward them by revealing his wrath against them? And that in the meantime, before the lifting of their divinely imposed blindness, they are living under a sentence of divine wrath?

REUBEN: You take 3:3 to be speaking about unbelief in the gospel. I think it refers to a more general "unfaithfulness" (ἀπιστία) of our people, our unworthiness before God, which we acknowledge every Sabbath in our synagogues when we pray for God's tender mercies. But no doubt it includes resistance to the gospel as well. Still, I fail to see your point.

CHARITON: My point is this: Paul clearly teaches that God's merciful righteousness is revealed in the gospel and applies to those who obey the gospel. The way God remains faithful to carnal Israel is by extending this mercy to them. Israelites who reject the covenant mercy of God are apostate. God is not obligated to be faithful to them, for they show that they are not true Israelites. If God brings down wrath on them, his faithfulness to his promises does not require that he also show them mercy beyond wrath, for he has already revealed his ultimate mercy to

Israel and to all people in the gospel. If his faithfulness requires that he save the whole of the faithless nation but not the whole of the gentiles, then he is favoring Israel and showing partiality. Perhaps you will say that, in Paul's view, God will save apostate Israel and show an equal mercy to all the nations. My point is that this extrapolation is not necessitated by Paul's logic. God's merciful faithfulness to Israel is satisfied by the gospel. If the nation spurns God's mercy and only a remnant have a share in the world to come, God's faithfulness is not proved false.

There is an ambiguity in the Greek of 3:3 (ἠπίστησάν τινες), where the NRSV, for example, translates, "What if some were unfaithful?" One could translate, "What if some have not believed?"[31] The use of the cognate verb πιστεύω in the preceding statement (v. 2) to mean "entrusted" suggests that the verb ἀπιστέω in v. 3 means "were not faithful," expressing the general sense of Paul's indictment against Israel in chapter 2. But the verb in 3:3 is also the common term in Paul for "believe." Hence many of Paul's original auditors would have heard an obvious reference to "not believing" (i.e., in the gospel message).

Chariton thinks that in Rom. 11:23, Paul uses the unqualified term ἀπιστία ("unbelief" or "unfaithfulness") to mean Jewish "unbelief" in the gospel. That is a justifiable conclusion. Elsewhere in Paul the related term ἄπιστος, when used substantively, appears to designate unbelievers. If we take ἀπιστία to mean rejection of the gospel, then Paul is saying that refusal to acknowledge the messiahship of Jesus is a denial of the oracles of God that find their fulfillment in Jesus. It would therefore count as covenant unfaithfulness, covenant falsehood, and covenant unrighteousness. Reuben does not dispute that unbelief in Jesus is covered by the term ἀπιστία in 3:3, but he rejects the suggestion that, in Paul's eyes, this puts the majority of Israelites outside the covenant(s).

REUBEN: Why do you speak of faithless Israel? Israel has a blind spot, owing to the partial hardening God has brought on his people to make room for the gentiles. Apart from this limited blindness, many, if not most, of our people trust God's mercy and show zeal for God's law. You depict Paul as a kind of Essene who thinks all Jews except those belonging to the Essene elect are in league with Belial. But Paul speaks like our own rabbis. He sorrows for his people; he knows their good zeal along with their blindness and sin. He also knows that God loves his people and will be merciful to them, for God's gifts and call are irrevocable.

Reuben derives the idea of a partial hardening from 11:25. The expression ἀπὸ μέρους ("in part") is perhaps most naturally taken adverbially: "A hardening has come in part on Israel."[32] The alternative is to construe it as an adjectival phrase modifying "Israel": "A hardening has come on Israel in part." If we adopt the adverbial interpretation, it seems most reasonable to conclude that the partial hardening pertains to Jewish response to the Christian gospel about Jesus, not to a general blindness toward righteousness and the meaning of the scriptures.

SIMEON: But Reuben, you are forgetting Paul's story of the olive tree (11:17–24). Those whom God has "cut out" of Israel must be apostates in Paul's eyes, people who no longer belong to the elect. Paul says that Jews who do not believe in the Messiah Jesus have been "cut out" of the olive tree, which is true Israel. That makes the mass of Jews apostates and false Israelites in Paul's eyes.

REUBEN: Then you do admit that the mass of unbelieving Jews once belonged to true Israel, before they were cut out?

CHARITON: No. Not all from Israel are Israel. Most of those from Israel are false Jews. They have enjoyed all the advantages of Israel, but now the revelation of God in Christ displays the truth about them. God cuts them out by giving them up to their own unbelief. God separates false Israel from true Israel. The true Jews are no longer to be found in the synagogue; they are in the churches of Christ.

REUBEN: Paul does not use the terms *true* and *false* to describe Jews or to distinguish two peoples called Israel.[33] The Jewish people are Israel. The tree stands for the riches of God's blessings, and its branches represent all who enjoy these riches. The roots of this tree are the patriarchs. Most of present-day Israel, to whom these promised blessings belong, has been temporarily removed from the tree, to make room for gentiles. This is why Paul sorrows over his kinspeople. He does not call them "false Jews." "They are Israelites," he says, "and to them belong the adoption, the glory, the covenants, the giving of the law, the worship, and the promises" (9:4). Or, as he says in his parable, they are the "natural branches" (11:21, 24).

Our dialogue partners next turn to Rom. 3:21–31. According to Simeon and Chariton, these verses show that, for Paul, there is no salvation for those who do not believe in Jesus. At least since the advent of Christ, the elect are limited to Christians. Reuben agrees that Paul's focus is Christians, but he objects to Simeon's and Chariton's attribution of exclusivism to Paul. He also disputes their interpretation of an ambiguous phrase, διὰ πίστεως Ἰησοῦ Χριστοῦ, which can mean either "through faith in Jesus Christ" or "through the faith of Jesus Christ" (3:22). Simeon

and Chariton think the expression refers to faith in Jesus. Reuben takes the
phrase to mean Jesus' own faithfulness.[34]

REUBEN: Paul says that the righteousness of God is for *all* who believe
    without distinction. You make it sound as if he says *only* for those
    who believe. But Paul is not speaking here directly about those
    who have *not* believed. He wants to vindicate his teaching that
    God justifies Jews and gentiles alike, apart from works of the law.
    To do that, he shows that redemption is through Jesus' own
    faithfulness unto death. The death of Jesus is atoning for the sins
    of the world. Generation after generation, God has made many
    provisions for the atonement of Israel's sins. Jesus is a provision
    made in these last days for the sins of Jews *and gentiles.*

CHARITON: You may believe that God offers Jesus to guarantee that the
    nation of Israel might have a share in the age to come. But
    Paul is thinking about another people of God: Jews and gen-
    tiles who believe in Jesus. The rest, including Israel according
    to the flesh, are lost.

REUBEN: Again, you draw out implications that are not required by what
    Paul says. Does Paul *deny* that the death of Jesus is effective for
    the nation of Israel when he *affirms* its effectiveness for both
    Jews and gentiles who believe the gospel of God's righteousness?

SIMEON: Then why does he not say here that the merciful righteousness
    of God is the justification of all Israel? Why does he attach the
    blessing of God's merciful righteousness so firmly and exclu-
    sively to faith in Jesus?

REUBEN: It is more firmly attached in your reading than in mine. I see only
    one reference here to believing the gospel, and there the point is
    not to exclude some but to include others. The other references to
    faith are to the atoning faith of Jesus. In the obedient faith of his
    Son, God confirms his faithfulness and merciful righteousness to
    Israel. But Paul does not yet speak of the irrevocable gifts and call
    to Israel, ratified by this faithfulness, for that might encourage
    some of his Jewish hearers to boast in their status as Israelites. Lest
    Jewish Christians boast in their election, signified by their works of
    the law, Paul says that all have sinned and lack the glory of God
    (3:23). And all are justified in the same way, by the same faithfulness
    of Jesus, who "has become a servant of the circumcised on behalf of
    the truth of God in order that he might confirm the promises given
    to the patriarchs and in order that the Gentiles might glorify God
    for his mercy" (15:8–9). We who have believed the gospel share in

the blessings of this justification in the present time. But the election of Israel still stands, and soon the Deliverer will come to "banish ungodliness from Jacob" (11:26) by removing Israel's sins in fulfillment of the covenant through the faithfulness of Jesus.

SIMEON: Ah, so the death of Jesus has not atoned for their sins! But let me ask you a question: While you are wringing unspoken possibilities from Paul's argument, do you also hear him implying that the whole world will be saved?

REUBEN: God promised Abraham that he would "inherit the world" (Rom. 4:13), meaning all the nations. The faith of Jesus reverses Adam's act of sin (5:12–21) and constitutes the whole seed of Adam as the inheritance of Abraham. In this way God's grace exercises dominion (5:21), when God has mercy on all (11:32).

CHARITON: No, no, for Paul the blessings of God belong only to those in Christ, those baptized into his death (6:1–14), those led by the Spirit (8:1–17). Outside Christ and the Spirit there is only slavery to sin, which brings death (6:23). As Paul has already said, in the judgment there will be wrath and fury for those who do not obey the truth (2:5, 8–9). And Jesus is the truth of God.

REUBEN: There can be mercy beyond wrath not only for Israel but for the gentiles too. In the inscrutable and unsearchable ways of God, the wrath that is even now being revealed against the world will be cut short by the mercy that God intends to show toward all. For just as God has brought a hardening on Israel, so God has shut up all the nations under sin, so that the whole world, including Israel, might be accountable to God and liable to God's wrathful judgment. But just as all Israel will be saved, so perhaps the whole world will be saved; for the unbelieving nations, like the nation of Israel, are God's enemies and yet are loved by God because of the patriarchs, and especially because of Abraham, through whom God promised that he would bless the nations.

SIMEON: You are overly fixed on 11:25–32; you want to make everything fit your interpretation of those few enigmatic verses. But I hear these verses very differently. According to Paul, there is a "fullness" of the Jews just as there is a "fullness" of the gentiles. A hardening, Paul says, has come on part of Israel. Numbered among the hardened are some who belong to this fullness. Not all of Paul's hardened kinspeople but only "some" of them belong to this elect, full number (11:14).

REUBEN: But Paul is clearly speaking of his kinsfolk who have not believed the gospel, for he speaks of them as "enemies" of the gospel and calls them "disobedient" (11:28, 31). These enemies and disobedient ones are to be saved. That can only mean that "all Israel" refers to our kinspeople as a whole, not to the church or to some small elect number of Jews. Not only that, Paul also says that "as regards election," these same enemies and disobedient ones are "beloved, for the sake of their ancestors" (11:28). That shows that the Jewish people as a whole are God's elect people Israel.

SIMEON: No, in 11:26 Paul is talking about elect Israel, not genealogical Israel. Many of this elect number of Israel, the "fullness" spoken of in 11:12, are now enemies toward the gospel but are beloved as far as their election is concerned and for the sake of their ancestors. Paul hopes to save "some," not "all," of his kinfolk (11:14).

REUBEN: Does Israel then mean something different in v. 25 than it does in v. 26?

SIMEON: As I see it, either Paul uses the name Israel in the way that he has already established in 9:6, where two different senses appear in a single verse, or Israel in both 11:25 and 11:26 means elect Israel. The point is, in the end, all who are destined to be part of Israel will be saved, including some of the Jews who have hardened themselves to the gospel, so that the number of Christian gentiles will not so greatly outweigh the number of Christian Jews, as it does now. But Paul is not envisioning the salvation of the entire nation of Israel. And even if he were hoping against hope that somehow all ethnic Israel might embrace the gospel, his hope could not be based on the idea that God must save the nation in fulfillment of any special promises to the Jews. Paul's fundamental view is that God is obliged to treat all nations alike. You think the nation is irrevocably elect. But a large part of genealogical Israel falls under the heading of "vessels of wrath," as Paul calls them in 9:22–24 where he distinguishes only some of the Jews as "vessels of mercy."

REUBEN: You turn Paul's "What if . . . ?" in 9:22 into an assertion. But when Paul speculates about whether God has prepared vessels of wrath, he is simply describing God's rights. He is not saying that God has, in fact, made any such vessels of wrath out of the majority of Israel. Rather, Paul puts his hearers in suspense and then resolves the question in chapter 11, where he says that God will save all Israel.[35]

CHARITON: You continue to insist that "all Israel" means carnal Israel, but this destroys Paul's argument, which demands that there be only an elect number, chosen by grace, within carnal Israel. Otherwise God would be favoring Jews over the gentiles.

REUBEN: It is not favoritism if he treats the gentile nations with the same boundless mercy.

SIMEON: You see, the problem with your interpretation is that you are forced to bring in this idea that all the gentiles will be saved. But Paul doesn't say that explicitly. It's an idea of your own that you use to help Paul out. Otherwise you would have to admit that the way you understand the salvation of all Israel contradicts what Paul has been saying about God's impartiality.

REUBEN: No, even if God does not save all the nations, God's impartiality is not impugned by the salvation of our nation. God will save our people according to his promise, to uphold his own righteousness, and not because of our works.

CHARITON: But if the Jews have the advantage of this promise, even though they are no more worthy than the gentiles, then God shows favoritism to them. But if "all Israel" is a full number of the elect within the Jewish nation, a divine selection made without regard to fleshly descent or to works of the law, then God has elected a full number from among the Jews just as he has done among the other nations.

REUBEN: It seems that you and Simeon also end up interpreting true Israel in a contradictory way. You say that according to 9:6–29 the present true Israel is the church, but that "all Israel" in 11:26 might be only elect Jews.

CHARITON: I don't insist on that. "All Israel" may be elect Jews; it may be the church of Jews and gentiles. In any case, there is a contradiction only if Paul ascribes partial treatment by God to the Jewish nation. And the idea of an irrevocable election of the whole nation of Israel, an election that no other nation enjoys, would amount to a gross form of divine partiality.

Methodological Analysis

Our fictional debate may strike many as containing, unwittingly, the proofs that Paul really does contradict himself in what he says about the identity and election of Israel and God's impartiality toward all. Rather than allow the most plausible interpretations of some parts of the letter (taken on their own terms) to justify less plausible interpretations of other parts of the letter (taken on their own terms), why not simply affirm the most plausible interpretation of each passage (taken on its own terms) and let those interpretations conflict with one another? There is nothing unreasonable about this approach, as long as it is not treated as the only reasonable way to construe the whole; for it is equally legitimate, in the face of plausible evidence to the contrary, (1) nevertheless to maintain the assumption that Paul has a coherent understanding of Israel, (2) on that assumption to construe some parts of the letter as clearer than others, (3) to use these "clearer" parts as interpretive keys, and (4) to produce a coherent Paul as probative evidence from the whole that one has rightly construed the parts.

A literary-critical analysis of how readers make sense of texts sheds light here. In an essay titled "Coherent Readers, Incoherent Texts," James R. Kincaid contrasts two current modes of critical reading, which he associates with Ralph Rader and Stanley Fish.[36] Rader begins with the assumption that "the mind by its nature actively seeks to impose meaning and to eliminate ambiguity in its encounters with the world," concluding that "so it must certainly be also with language."[37] In the reading and interpreting of literary texts, this means, for Rader, that we take pleasure in grasping the single, overall intention and resulting pattern in a work and then are permitted "to eliminate in the act of reading any potential incoherence and ambiguities which cannot be resolved within our appreciation of the coherence of the whole."[38] By contrast, Fish celebrates a way of reading that entails incessant revision of interpretation and eschews the thought that there might be a single, overall coherence to a work. Kincaid comments that "Fish's reader, assuming indeterminacy, is quick to abandon his search for a single ordering system in the face of contradictory signals," but "Rader's is just as quick and ingenious in finding means for subordinating or ignoring these signals."[39]

Kincaid argues further that there is a limited number of basic patterns of interpretation for any literary text. Interpreters eventually discover these patterns and recycle them, generation after generation, with various modifications and fresh arguments.[40] Kincaid has in mind the way in which the codes of genre admit a limited but also irreducible range of interpretations for literary texts, but his observation can be generalized for other interpretive situations, including the construal of ambiguity in argument. To read as coherently as we can is to produce a "reading," but more than one such reading is possible. Still, the number of plausible readings is bounded. The history of interpretation eventually reveals a limited number of patterns that can be reasonably imposed on an argument to give it coherence.

The possibility of multiple valid readings owes to a number of factors, one of which is the relation of the part to the whole. This problematic relationship can produce a set of interminable hermeneutic circles, because a text is both a linear-temporal unfolding and a semantic space. Consider, for example, Romans 1—4, taken as a part. Regarded in artificial isolation from the rest of Romans, these first four chapters appear to teach some version of ecclesial Israelism. We can therefore say that the letter's linear manifestation is a strong warrant for interpreting the rest of the letter as equating the church with true Israel. This does not mean that things said later in the letter have no power to overthrow the impression of ecclesial Israelism in chapters 1—4, but it does mean that Romans is structured in a way that puts the burden of proof on those who would argue that Paul affirms some form of national Israelism.

But can "all Israel" in Rom. 11:26 be interpreted within its immediate context to mean anything other than the *nation* of Israel? Certainly, if we possessed a letter consisting only of Romans 11, together with a fitting opening and closing, and if we interpreted this letter on its own terms, the *only* definition of Israel's identity and destiny that it could reasonably be said to support would be some version of national Israelism. As part of the whole of Romans, however, the strong appearance of national Israelism in chapter 11 stands under a question mark. Nevertheless, Romans 11 also raises a question mark against the strong impression that ecclesial Israelism or elect remnant Israelism is taught by the preceding ten chapters.

These two sections of Romans, taken on their own and in isolation from each other, support opposing interpretations of the identity and destiny of the Jewish nation. Since each section forms part of the other's epistolary context, we must compare them and seek to construe them so that they harmonize coherently or at least pose a coherent paradox. Otherwise we have no choice but to say that the two sections contradict each other, in which case we can go on to explore the nature and significance of that contradiction. A structuralist model of a work's meaning suggests that parts acquire their meaning only in relation to one another. When we treat Romans 1—4 and Romans 11 apart from each other, we get different interpretive results from those we produce when we view these sections in relation to each other.

But relating the two is not simply a matter of thinking them separately and then together until our interpretations of them as parts adjust into a unified conception of their coherence with each other. We must take account of the unfolding of the letter, which justifies treating prior stages of discussion as preparation for what follows. As a general rule, what comes later ought to be construed *in the light of* what comes earlier, which presupposes that we have understood what comes earlier on its own terms and without recourse to what follows. On this view, the structural model of a spatial interaction between a work's parts must be brought under a rhetorical model of linear unfolding.

Nevertheless, to subordinate the spatial model rigidly to the temporal model is too simple. In a certain sense, rereading converts texts into "timeless spaces" by making endings present in, and thus contiguous to, beginnings. In addition, rhetorical strategies for producing meaning often involve disclosure devices that establish later parts as the hermeneutical keys to earlier parts. If Romans 11 introduces a surprise disclosure that warrants a rereading of earlier parts of the letter,[41] then Romans provides an excellent example of why we must keep the spatial and the linear models in tension with each other. That is what competent readers do when they reread and ask themselves, for instance, whether they should revise their understanding of the beginning in the light of their interpretation of the (now remembered) ending or revise that interpretation of the ending in the light of what they are seeing afresh in the beginning. The range of plausible readings warranted for Romans includes taking Rom. 11:25–32 as a late disclosure that justifies a remarkable revision of what a reader would otherwise conclude about Paul's view of the Jewish people in Romans 1—10. On this reading, the Jewish nation turns out to have been true Israel all along. But this reasonable interpretation, which attributes some form of national Israelism to Paul, competes with other reasonable interpretations of the identity and destiny of the Jewish people in Romans.

Furthermore, to attend to the text in a way that makes it "one" does not necessarily mean making it coherent. Heikki Räisänen, for example, argues that Romans 9—11 is substantially incoherent.[42] In many cases, however, one cannot prove that a text is incoherent any more than one can prove that it is coherent. What one *can* do is construe the text in reasonable ways, some of which may be reasonable ways of finding it incoherent. The matter is further complicated by the fact that some forms of ostensible incoherence can be esteemed as virtues. For example, E. Elizabeth Johnson insists that throughout Romans 9—11 Paul achieves a "balanced tension" between God's faithfulness to (ethnic) Israel and God's impartial treatment of all.[43] While Räisänen sees this same tension as a muddled contradiction, Johnson writes about it in a way that reflects her delight in Paul's accomplishment: "This means that God's impartiality cannot nullify God's covenant promises to Israel, but neither can God's faithfulness be construed as loyalty that can somehow be manipulated by human behavior or identity. God's mercy is just and God's justice is merciful."[44]

Further light is shed on these questions by considering an essay by Timothy Bahti.[45] Bahti provides a very helpful discussion of ambiguity and indeterminacy as concepts that carry different meanings, depending on whether they are conceived within the framework of New Criticism or within the more or less common framework of current approaches that stress the indeterminacy of texts. For New Criticism, ambiguity in a literary text is an indeterminacy to be resolved by the critic, for example, through an attribution of paradox to the work. In more recent criticism, indeterminacy is an unresolvable property of both text and interpretation, because texts are seen as having no meaning apart from interpretation and yet as warranting (often, if not always) opposing interpretations. Thus "for New Criticism texts were fundamentally ambiguous and interpretations fundamentally were not," while "today texts are ambiguous and interpretations are indeterminate."[46] Bahti uses this insight to argue that New Criticism tends to misrepresent literature ("the poet's truth" becomes "the critic's falsehood") by not letting interpretation circulate through equally possible readings without being resolved into a single understanding.[47]

Justifiable readings constitute what may be described as *the full range of rigorously plausible readings.*[48] This range includes, on the one hand, each reading that grasps, on the basis of a reasonable use of the cultural-linguistic lexicon, an overall coherence (or logic) in a work by resolving all ambiguities in ways that are consistent with that coherence. On the other hand, it also includes readings (again, carried out on the basis of a reasonable use of the cultural-linguistic lexicon) that attribute contradiction to the text. Where a text is judged to admit plausible interpretations of both the first type (attribution of coherence) and the second type (attribution of incoherence), those of the first type ought, in principle, to be given precedence over those of the second. In such cases, one should judge the attribution of incoherence as falling outside the plausible range, since it is not reasonable to construe a text as incoherent when it admits a coherent and plausible interpretation. But in many exegetical debates, all of the plausible coherent readings entail construals of some parts of the text that would be judged implausible *were it not for the fact that they make possible a coherent reading that is otherwise based on very plausible ways of interpreting most of the text.* In such cases, the attribution of incoherence might also be plausible, in which case it would fall within the reasonable range of interpretive arguments.

It has not been my purpose to argue that everything Paul writes admits more than one plausible construal. It has long been recognized, however, that there is something very malleable about Paul. Not only has Paul been claimed for almost every conceivable cause in the West, but he also seems to invite contrary uses. The task, then, is to demonstrate as clearly as possible what interpretations are ruled out and what remain viable options. In this respect, the historical approach to Paul has made considerable progress, not only by liberating Paul from dogmatic eisegesis but also through the critical self-correction that marks historical study as a science. But some protean features remain and will remain, not simply because we know too little but also because we have learned so much. This, too, is a legacy of historical criticism: the unwitting upshot of the work of so many able hands, all endeavoring to establish the single, correct meaning and achieving ensemble a definitive proof that, in case after case, more than one rigorously plausible interpretation of Paul's apparent intent will exist.

Thus we can see just how Paul's text structures Israel as an ambiguous sign in the smaller and larger arguments of the letter. While we will never know Paul's communicational intent in this matter, we can establish the limited range of interpretations that his text warrants. What we are to do with this knowledge is a question for the next chapter.

2

Hermeneutical Election

"We all seek the center that will allow the senses to rest," Frank Kermode observes, "at any rate for one interpreter, at any rate for one moment."[1] When it comes to momentous uses of scripture, we may experience our desire for that center as a necessity, which may beget in us the illusion of exegetical closure where it is unwarranted. Or we may discover that "it is much easier to study than to decide," as Giovanni Battista Montini confessed when contemplating the papers on the question of birth control that confronted him in the first days of his tenure as Pope Paul VI.[2] The very weight of the decision may become a temptation to resist closure.

Interpretation of the canonical Romans involves making and defending interpretive choices about plausible ways to bring Paul's sense to rest for the use of his text by a Christian community. In one way or another, such choices involve the "will." This chapter explores the role of the interpretive will, beginning with a rhetorical analysis of certain features of Paul's argument in Romans 9—11. This leads to a more general hermeneutical discussion of the interpretive will and hermeneutical responsibility. The chapter concludes with a reflection on making interpretive choices about the canonical identity of Israel in a post-Holocaust situation.

Choosing the Identity of
Israel in Romans 9—11

Rhetorical questions usually imply their own answers or else receive immediate answers from those who pose them. But a rhetorical question can also initiate a moment of co-deliberation with one's audience, thus producing a degree of rhetorical drama. To formulate an example: What if Paul, wishing to justify the absolute rights of God over humanity, were to assert the idea of double predestination—the election of some human beings for temporary use and then destruction, the election of others for mercy and ultimate salvation? To pose such a question is to create a bit of suspense and at the same time to raise the expectation that one is about to argue for what the question suggests—in this case, what it suggests about Paul's apparent intent. If this chapter were to fulfill that expectation, we could describe my question, in rhetorical terms, as co-deliberation resolved by an anticipated sequel. But I might go on to surprise my readers.

First Impressions

At first glance, Rom. 9:22ff. suggests that Paul indeed asserts the election of some human beings for temporary use and then destruction, of others for mercy and ultimate salvation. Moreover, first impressions are sometimes correct. Sometimes it is only the will to discover other, more attractive interpretive possibilities that leads interpreters to reject prima facie evidence and construct implausibly elaborate, alternative readings.

Paul writes, "What if God, desiring to show wrath and demonstrate his power, has endured with much patience vessels of wrath made for destruction—and that in order to make known the wealth of his glory to vessels of mercy, which he has prepared beforehand for glory?" (Rom. 9:22–23; my translation). It has been rightly pointed out that Paul's topic here is not predestination but the question of God's covenant with Israel.[3] It is also true, as commentators now like to emphasize, that Paul does not say that the vessels of wrath are Jews, Israel according to the flesh. One thing seems clear: Pharaoh is a vessel of wrath. But perhaps there is no need to speculate any further, that is, to draw the inference that Paul is dividing fleshly Israel into two categories: those destined for eschatological destruction and those destined for eschatological salvation.

Nevertheless, when Paul speaks of vessels prepared by God for different destinies, and when he goes on to identify the vessels of mercy prepared for glory as including "us whom he has called, not from the Jews only but also from the Gentiles," it is reasonable to conclude that the vessels of wrath constitute an analogous and opposing group of people, those to whom God will not be merciful and who have not been fashioned for glory. Moreover, the mass of Israelites according to the flesh who have not accepted the gospel message spring to mind as the obvious candidates for inclusion in this group, along with the gentile world as a whole. To draw this inference as Paul's apparent intent is not strictly demanded by his argumentative logic; but then, neither is avoiding it. On the contrary, the text invites the interpretation that, in the course of explaining God's justice toward Israel, Paul affirms a doctrine of double predestination.[4]

Connecting
Romans 9 and 11

C. H. Dodd recognized the apparent implication of a double predestination and balked, calling Rom. 9:20–21 "the weakest point in the whole epistle" and concluding from the "obscure" quality of Paul's logic in 9:22–23
that Paul is "embarrassed by the position he has taken up."[5] James Dunn
finds more care and subtlety in Paul's argument. He thinks there is an important nuance of difference between "made" ("for destruction") and "prepared beforehand" ("for glory"). Noting that Paul uses "make" (καταρτίζω)
and not "pre-make" (προκαταρτίζω) for the vessels of wrath, Dunn maintains that Paul "very likely" intends to avoid the idea that these vessels are
prepared for destruction through an originating act of divine predestination.
Instead, the divine wrath works out, in the present time, a suitable preparation of these vessels for destruction—suitable because they have already chosen for themselves the destiny God assigns to them, like humanity as de-
picted in Rom. 1:18–32.[6]

Against Dunn's interpretation, one may note that there is no hint elsewhere in the argumentative context of any such differentiation. God loves
Jacob and hates Esau before they are born, before they have done either
good or evil (9:11–13). Apparently, no one can resist God's will (9:19).
That prompts the question of why God still holds people accountable if
they become only what the divine will makes them. Here is Paul's oppor-
tunity to qualify by clarifying that at least in the case of dis-election, of exclusion from mercy, human beings first exclude themselves before God excludes them. But Paul's answer suggests just the opposite. The potter has
absolute rights over the clay, "to make *from the same lump* one vessel for
honorable use and another for dishonorable use" (9:21; my translation and
emphasis). The "What if. . ." sentence (v. 22) immediately follows. Thus
the flow of the argument is a strong warrant for construing "made"
(κατηρτισμένα) and "prepared beforehand" (προητοίμασεν) as synony-
mous, taking the second of these as a sharper expression of the thought introduced by the first. While Dunn's interpretation is not ruled out, the immediate context does not establish it as likely.

At this point, however, someone might rightly object that I am forgetting Paul's prophecy concerning fleshly Israel in Romans 11:

> For I do not want you to be ignorant, brothers, of this mystery, so that you
> do not become conceited. A hardening in part has come over Israel, until the
> full number of the gentiles comes in; and thus all Israel will be saved. As it is
> written:
>
> > The Deliverer will come from Zion;
> > he will turn away ungodliness from Jacob.

> And this will be my covenant with them,
> when I take away their sins.
>
> From the standpoint of the gospel, they are enemies for your sake; but from the standpoint of election they are beloved for the sake of the fathers, for the gifts and call of God are irrevocable.
>
> (11:25–29; my translation)

If "all Israel will be saved" (11:26) because "the gifts and call of God are irrevocable" (11:29), then the mass of Israelites numbered among the vessels of wrath turn out to be foreordained as vessels of mercy after all. This interpretation of Rom. 11:26 makes Dunn's construal of 9:22 more plausible. Perhaps Paul deliberately leaves some room in the language of 9:22 for the surprising revelation he plans to make in chapter 11.

That is quite possible, but two cautionary observations are in order. First, if what Paul affirms about Israel in Romans 11 comes as a surprise, that in itself shows how strong the countervailing reading of Romans 9 is. The idea that all carnal Israel, the nation as a whole, is to be saved confronts the reader as a surprise precisely because Paul's argument up to that point has created the impression that fleshly Israel as a whole is not destined for mercy. Second, if chapters 1—10 of Romans, considered apart from Romans 11, have, at critical points, given the strong appearance of arguing that the concept of elect Israel does not include but actually excludes the idea that the nation as a whole is destined for mercy, then the weight of this very (or even most) plausible way of construing chapters 1—10 by themselves ought to give us pause when we reach what looks like an affirmation in 11:25–29 of an irrevocable election of national Israel.[7]

Rhetorical Tricks

The opinion that Paul is indeed speaking of the nation—so-called empirical Israel—in announcing the future salvation of "all Israel" (11:26) is now widely held by Pauline scholars. But given Paul's assertions of divine impartiality toward Jews and gentiles,[8] the idea of an irrevocable election of carnal Israel poses a problem. How can Paul hold together divine impartiality (universalism) and the irrevocable election of Israel (particularism) in Romans?[9] As noted in chapter 1, some interpreters think that Paul fails to manage this with any logical consistency.[10] Others speak of a coherent "dynamic tension" in Paul's argument[11] or of a deeper unity beneath the apparent surface tensions.[12] All recognize how strongly Romans weighs in favor of radical divine impartiality and against any traditional conceptions of Jewish national particularism. In fact, if it were not for chapter 11, there would be no debate about how divine impartiality and the divine election of Israel hang together logically in Romans, for there would be no reason to assert that Paul affirms an irrevocable election of carnal Israel. The argument of chapter 11 interjects that idea, which justi fies the characterization of this turn in Paul's argument as a surprise.

This is not to gainsay Richard Hays's impressive demonstration of how a tacit presence of scriptural voices functions in Romans 9 to intimate God's merciful loyalty to the nation of Israel. Speaking of Romans as a whole, Hays astutely observes that "the letter's rhetorical structure lures the reader into expecting Israel's final condemnation," while "the later chapters undercut such an expectation."[13] Hays adapts literary critic John Hollander's theory of intertextual "echoes"[14] to show how readers familiar with the original contexts of the scripture passages that Paul quotes can discover meaningful operations of ideas from those contexts in Paul's arguments. In a work of literature, echoes of other works "can lie in the unstated or suppressed (transumed) points of resonance between the two texts."[15] Hollander calls this "metalepsis." To interpret a metalepsis, one must recover the suppressed material from the first (earlier) text and discern its signifying contribution to the second text. Hays looks for unstated or suppressed points of resonance between Paul's arguments and the original contexts of the scripture quotations and allusions that figure so importantly in those arguments.

In Romans 9, Paul uses two quotations from Hosea to express God's election of the gentiles:

> Those who were not my people I will call "my
>   people,"
> and her who was not beloved I will call
>   "beloved."
> And in the very place where it was said to them,
>   "You are not my people,"
> there they shall be called children of the living
>   God.
> (Hos. 2:23 and 1:10 [Hebrew 2:1] in Rom. 9:25–26)

It looks as if Paul is denying the literal sense of Hos. 2:23 and 1:10,[16] which refer not to gentiles but to Jews. As Hays skillfully shows, however, echoes of the literal sense of Hosea can be plausibly construed as part of the undercurrent of Paul's argumentation, where they suggest to the reader who knows scripture well that God will yet be gracious to carnal Israel.

Wayne Meeks concurs. Building on the work of Hays, Meeks evaluates Paul's uses of scripture in Romans 9—10 as provocative *misreadings*.[17] Nevertheless, Meeks suggests, the knowing reader hears the literal sense of the Hosea texts as an echo of a scripture sense that Paul will honor in Roman 11. Paul *suppresses* the plain sense of the scripture texts he quotes, holding that sense "in reserve" until a later point in his argument.[18]

Meeks proposes further that this rhetorical strategy is part of a theological strategy. Paul "plays tricks" on his readers in order to confront them with "the trick that God has played on Israel" and thus to teach them what it means to trust an unpredictable God.[19] God's trick is a seeming betrayal of Israel, which troubles Christian confidence: "for if Christians are to accept Paul's assurance that 'nothing will be able to separate us from the love of God', they must face the fact that Jews have rested upon exactly the same assurance, and the radicality of Paul's claims throughout the letter so far has undermined that assurance."[20] Paul's argument in Romans 1—10 leaves the impression that God is not bound by any promises made to ethnic Israel. But in Rom. 11:25–29, Paul discloses the "mystery" that "all Israel will be saved" because "the gifts and call of God are irrevocable." Paul's aim, Meeks says, is to establish God's trustworthiness without denying that God has acted in Christ in unpredictable ways. The same divine love that once chose the Jewish people now seeks out another people, against all expectation, yet not by breaking faith with Israel. Thus, Paul's rhetorical craftiness imitates God's craftiness toward Israel and does so with the same pedagogical aim.

But who, then, is the reader on whom Paul plays tricks? Whatever "echoes of scripture" readers may hear in chapter 9, they have no basis for thinking that Paul, by means of tacit voices of scripture, wishes to affirm God's unfailing loyalty to Israel—until they reach chapter 11. Hence, the most sophisticated reader must also be deceived on a first reading of Romans 9, for to be a "knowing reader" requires not merely hearing the echoes but recognizing that they serve a constitutive function in Paul's argument. One must discern that in suppressing the plain sense of scripture, Paul is indeed "holding it in reserve" for a later affirmation. But only the surprise disclosure in Romans 11 and its further elaboration 15:7–13 provide a warrant for imagining that this is how we are to take Paul's uses of Hosea in Romans 9.

Meeks uses the literary-critical term "peripeteia" ("turning point" or "reversal") to describe the dramatic rhetorical function of Paul's declaration in 11:26 that "all Israel will be saved." Since 11:26 is also the moment when the reader is undeceived by Paul, we should call it an instance of "recognition" (anagnorisis).[21] This leads us to a paradox in interpretive method. To show that a surprising peripeteia exists in Romans 11, one must do two things: (1) defend as very plausible the deceived reader's reading up to the point of disclosure, and (2) defend an interpretation of 11:25–29 that shows it to be a surprise reversal of this deceived reader's reading. The first of these tasks is not difficult. But to the extent that we succeed at this, we also strengthen the grounds for suspecting that the "surprise" in chapter 11 may be a mirage. Perhaps Paul is not, after all, speaking about the *nation* of Israel in 11:26 but rather has in view the church of Jews and gentiles as the "all Israel" of the new eschatological time. Or perhaps he is thinking of an elect Israel within carnal Israel, whose full number constitutes all true Israel.

These alternative interpretations of 11:26 do not lack able defenders. N. T. Wright, for example, argues very plausibly that "all Israel" in 11:26 is the new community of Jews and gentiles in Christ.[22] And François Refoulé shows how cogently one can construe "all Israel" as an elect remnant composed exclusively of Jews within an otherwise dis-elect nation of Israel.[23] Both interpretations fit better with 11:12–14, where Paul seems to hope for the salvation of only "some" of his kinfolk. Moreover, either of these two interpretations eliminates the problem of how Paul can affirm the irrevocable election of carnal Israel after everything else he has done in the letter: specifically, arguing so emphatically for divine impartiality; insisting that there is no distinction between Jew and gentile; redefining circumcision in a way that allows physically uncircumcised gentiles to be "true Jews" (2:25–29); redefining election in a way that disconnects it from fleshly identity (9:6ff.); insinuating that the Jewish people stand under God's wrath (3:1–8);[24] and suggesting that, except for a few elect ones, the Jewish nation as a whole belongs among the vessels of wrath prepared for destruction (9:22ff.). Although a majority of scholars now think that "all Israel" is the Jewish nation as a whole, whose election is irrevocable, no satisfactory answer has been given to the objection that this makes God partial in a way that contradicts the whole tenor of the first ten chapters of Romans.[25]

Co-deliberation
and Suspense

Paul's apparent intent is ambiguous enough in Romans to allow for more than one critically justifiable interpretation of what he says about the divine election of "Israel." This plasticity places interpretive options before our will, and we choose. We engage in hermeneutical election. As it happens, Paul himself, in Rom. 11:11ff., encourages us to do just that: to elect for or against the election or dis-election of carnal Israel.

Speaking of "blind" carnal Israel, Paul asks, "Now if their stumbling brings about wealth for the world and if their defeat brings about wealth for the Gentiles, how much more their fullness [πλήρωμα]?" (11:12). This question asks the auditor to contemplate such an inclusion, and the mention of benefits ("wealth") appeals to the will. Thus, before Paul confirms or disconfirms the prospect of a fullness of carnal Israel, he bids his hearers to entertain that possibility and to decide whether they find it attractive or not. To be sure, Paul also *encourages* them, but his question invites them to judge for themselves, at least for the moment.

That moment stretches out, however. Paul does not go on immediately to indicate whether or not he is prophesying the full inclusion of his kinfolk. Paul's next statement seems to hedge: "Inasmuch then as I am an apostle to the Gentiles, I glorify my ministry in order to make my own people jealous, and thus save some of them" (11:12b–13). Or does Paul simply mean that his ministry may win "some," while he hopes that in the end God will win all? Paul's question about the fate of Israel creates rhetorical suspense, which ancient rhetoricians called *sustentatio*, produced through co-deliberation (*communicatio*) with one's audience.[26]

Quintilian illustrates co-deliberation with an example from Cicero's *Against Verres* (*Institutio Oratoria* 9.2.22). Recounting the dishonorable record of Verres, under whose jurisdiction the province of Sicily fell, Cicero tells how Verres managed a case involving an alleged slave conspiracy in Sicily. Intimating that his audience expects to hear how Verres exploited the case to his own financial advantage, Cicero asks, "What then? What do you think? Perhaps you expect to hear of some theft or plunder?" (*Against Verres* 5.5.10). These co-deliberative questions create suspense. Quintilian observes that the sequel, which resolves such a suspense, can take one of two forms: it may confirm an expectation raised by the moment of co-deliberation, or it may bring a surprise (a παράδοξον).

The device of "suspension" is mentioned by modern rhetorical theorists Ch. Perelman and L. Olbrechts-Tyteca in their presentation of a "new rhetoric."[27] These authors observe that speakers sometimes pose a rhetorical question to which they give a hypothetical answer, usually one they will go on to reject.[28] Adapting a speech to one's audience sometimes calls for such hypothetical detours. The speaker may need to treat some arguments before others can be effectively introduced.[29] Quintilian's example from Cicero, however, suggests a somewhat different purpose. Suspense serves Cicero's larger argument not through a logic of order, adapted to the particular assumptions of the audience, but through a psychology of order, which conditions the auditors' disposition so that the sequel will have maximum psychological effect. Rhetorical suspense works at the affective level to further the purposes of the larger argument. Co-deliberation with suspense encourages the audience to entertain a possibility, and a strategy of suspense issuing in a surprise must encourage the audience down a plausible but false track of expectation.

Although suspense has been explored only minimally as a device of argument, it has been much analyzed as a poetic device. In his *Handbuch der literarischen Rhetorik*, Heinrich Lausberg, for example, makes no mention of suspense as a technique of argumentation, but he does treat it as a dramatic device.[30] In narrative and drama, suspense issuing in surprise often takes the form of recognition (anagnorisis). The true identity of a character or the truth about an action is disclosed, resolving the suspense in a way that subverts expectations. In Quintilian's example from Cicero, the disclosure functions dramatically like a recognition scene, but the purpose is not simply to produce an aesthetic effect; it is also to persuade. The aesthetic and the argumentative effects are nevertheless interconnected here. The drama of the suspense followed by Cicero's disclosure of an even more serious crime than "theft or plunder"[31] strengthens the rhetorical effect of the speech.

Since a strategy of suspense issuing in a surprise must lure the audience down a plausible but false track of expectation, it can be rhetorically risky to use suspense with a surprise sequel in a complex argument. If there is unclarity in the sequel or if the sequel is not clearly marked as such, auditors may miss—or at least misconstrue—the intended resolution. If the designed false impression is given too much strength, and if the eventual surprise sequel is not clearly indicated or is stated in a way that is open to misinterpretation, then the device may fail. By the same token, from the standpoint of the interpreter, to look for subtle surprise sequences may lead one to find them in the text where they were, in fact, not intended by the author. Nevertheless, it might still be possible to show that such a doubtful surprise resolution is a plausible reading of the author's apparent intent.

Co-deliberation and Suspense
in Romans 11:11–32

In Rom. 11:11–32, Paul asks his readers to contemplate not only the possibility but also the advantages of a full inclusion of the Jewish people in salvation, the advantages being more benefits for his Christian audience. In v. 15, Paul escalates but also complicates the suspense by asking, "For if their rejection is the reconciliation of the world, what will their acceptance be but life from the dead!" The mention of "life from the dead" heightens the drama, but now it is not so evident that Paul envisions a full inclusion of all ethnic Israel. Perhaps the inclusion of some but not all of his kinfolk will suffice to precipitate maximal eschatological blessing for the elect. Perhaps the word "fullness" (πλήρωμα) used in v. 12 means only the filling up of an elect number of Israelites and not the inclusion of the nation as a whole.

The argumentative context certainly admits this way of construing 11:15: "Now I am speaking to you Gentiles. Inasmuch then as I am an apostle to the Gentiles, I glorify my ministry in order to make my own people jealous, and thus save some of them" (11:13–14). Moreover, if we use this passage as a model for understanding the prophecy of the salvation of all Israel (in 11:26), we may draw the following interpretive conclusions. When, in God's providence, the full number of the gentiles is complete, the still-hardened nation of Israel will be made jealous (according to the prophecy of Deuteronomy) and *some of the hardened Israelites* will accept the gospel and be saved.[32] The number of these Israelites is known only to God. Together with the elect remnant, that number will make up the "full number" (πλήρωμα) of elect Israelites. "All Israel" refers to this number, or it may designate the elect people made up of the full number of the gentiles and the full number of the Jews.[33] Or we might think of true Israel as the elect of genealogical Israel blending with the new people of God made up of Jews and gentiles.

John Chrysostom, who did not want to find any promise of the salvation of all carnal Israel in Romans 11, discovered a warrant for lower expectations (Chrysostom, *Homily 19 on Romans*). He took all Paul's statements about a future inclusion of Israel as expressions of mere possibilities, designed as rhetorical "conciliations" to Jewish auditors. And certainly Chrysostom is correct that, at least in vv. 11–24, Paul does not explicitly affirm that all carnal Israel will be saved. Nevertheless, Paul is not merely throwing sops to Jews but is insisting that his gentile hearers contemplate the possibility of the full inclusion of the Jewish people. In so doing, he practices the rhetorical device of co-deliberation, which creates suspense—a suspense resolved somewhat cryptically in 11:25ff.

Co-deliberation and
Suspense in Rom. 9:22–23:
Reconnecting Romans 9 and 11

There are, in fact, two instances of co-deliberation in Romans. Besides the rhetorical moment in Romans 11 that we have just examined, there is an instance of co-deliberation in 9:22ff., the passage with which we began. Paul's "What if . . . ?" asks his audience to entertain a possibility. A moment of suspense materializes, but in this case it seems almost immediately to evaporate. The argument, in its immediate development, produces the impression that Paul meant his "What if . . . ?" as an "Indeed. . . ."[34]

But suppose that, despite appearances, the suspense in 9:22 is not immediately resolved but has a surprise sequel—one that does not appear until the second co-deliberation with suspense in 11:11ff.? In that case Paul is being very clever, perhaps too clever. He succeeds so well at setting up a false impression in 9:22ff., and he delays so long before introducing his surprise sequel, that his audience can find reason to doubt that the two rhetorical moments are to be connected. Nevertheless, those readers who make the connection will conclude that 9:22 is not declarative but deliberative. Paul's "What if . . . ?" is a hypothetical that does not assert what God has done but invites Paul's audience to consider what God has a right to do. If 9:22ff. is an instance of co-deliberation and suspense, issuing at length in a surprise sequel, then perhaps the Israelites over whom Paul sorrows in 9:2–3 are *not* included among the vessels of wrath, despite what the immediate context in chapter 9 seems to imply. In that case, one also has reason to doubt that there *are* any objects of wrath at all. Perhaps God has not fitted any for destruction. Or, without doubting that God has prepared vessels of wrath, including the Israelites over whom Paul sorrows, one may conclude from the surprise disclosure that God will not bring these vessels to the destruction that befits them.

This gets us, by a different route, to an interpretation close to Dunn's construal of 9:22 (see above). It would be important, however, that the hypothetical in 9:22ff. still be taken seriously. Paul's question asks the auditor to deliberate, and it engenders deliberation by being provocative. To eliminate what is provocative—for example, by purporting to establish that Paul is not lumping Israel together with the enemy of Israel, Pharaoh, that he is not suggesting that Israel and Pharaoh might be like two pieces of clay worked up for immolation in a vast display of divine wrath and power—to rule out from deliberation the entertainment of such possibilities is to ignore what Paul's language *does* here, the way it encourages the reader down a track that, arguably, turns out to be false, but which is not arguably false except on the basis of a particular interpretation of 11:11–36.

In summary, the preceding analysis suggests that the co-deliberative moment in 11:11ff. reactivates what had seemed to be only a momentary suspense—a quickly, if only implicitly, resolved suspense in 9:22ff. Nevertheless, since the arrival in chapter 11 of the proposed surprise reversal is so delayed, and since the connection between 11:11–32 and 9:22ff. is not explicit, one is not compelled to take 11:11ff. as a sequel to 9:22ff.

Co-deliberation as a
Hermeneutical Locale

Before asserting the salvation of all Israel in Rom. 11:26, Paul speaks of the benefits that would accrue if his kinfolk were saved: more "wealth" for the world, even "life from the dead!" Thus, before affirming that all Israel will be saved, Paul seeks to cultivate in his audience a *will* to the salvation of all carnal Israel. This also means that before Paul confirms anything, he first asks his audience to discover through co-deliberation whether they have a will to believe in the salvation of all Israel. In their own desire, have they elected for or against a divine election of carnal Israel? And if they have no heart to believe in the salvation of the Jewish nation, is there anything in what Paul says to change their minds?

Granted that Paul does provide reasons for such a change of mind, those reasons do not, by themselves, establish Paul's own views about the election and destiny of carnal Israel. They suggest his desire, not his teaching. And auditors unfriendly to Paul might even take the unclarity of his argument as a whole as a sign of deliberate political obfuscation, warranting doubt about the sincerity of the posture he adopts toward the nation in 9:1–5, 10:1, and 11:11ff. But even charitable readers may be uncertain how to construe Paul's argument. Does Paul mean to say that carnal Israel as a whole will be saved or only that a salvation of the whole nation cannot be ruled out? And in either case, on what grounds would they be saved? According to an inviolable divine election of the nation? By saving faith in Jesus Christ? Both of these? Moreover, if Paul's teaching about divine impartiality seems to contradict the notion of a special election of the Jewish people, is it reasonable to conclude that Paul affirms that special election when one can also reasonably construe his arguments in a way that does not require this conclusion?

If Paul's original auditors were perplexed by what he says about Israel in Romans 9—11, they at least had the promise of a personal visit by Paul to clear things up (15:24). For us that visit never arrives, just as one might say that it never arrives for the implied reader, who stands for the range of justifiable ways to construe Paul's argument without the empirical Paul's further help. No matter how many times we reread Romans, we remain, figuratively speaking, always in the place of co-deliberation, which thus becomes a trope of our hermeneutical situation. In that hermeneutical space, we must resolve for ourselves a semantic suspense that neither Paul himself nor his text can resolve for us. Standing in the place of the implied readers of 11:11ff., we, too, must choose what we want the destiny of Paul's kinfolk to be.

Co-deliberation in perpetual suspense invites an interpretive activity that might be described as the hermeneutical counterpart of self-involving linguistic acts.[35] When texts warrant *personal* decisions about their subject matter as a basis for interpretation, they justify exegesis as a self-involving act. In one respect this suggestion agrees with a widely acknowledged general rule of interpretation, namely, that one must attain an "insider's" point of view. One does so by joining, at least for the moment, the world of the text, which entails a kind of hypothetical assent to the perspective of the text. This act resembles joining a community in order to carry out an ethnography.[36] It is also akin to the "willing suspension of disbelief" that goes with reading a novel.[37] Moreover, it evokes the old distinction between a sacred hermeneutic (*hermeneutica sacra*) and an ordinary or general hermeneutic (*hermeneutica profana*), the former often being conceived as requiring a special form of self-involvement, specifically, being in Christ, guidance by the Spirit, and use of the "rule of faith" (*analogia fidei*) as a hermeneutical guide.[38] While co-deliberation in perpetual suspension does not require the use of a sacred hermeneutic, it does warrant a self-involving decision about how to describe the meaning of the text.[39]

I have characterized this warrant as an invitation, but one might define it more precisely as an oblique command. Must an interpreter heed a text in order rightly to interpret it? An implication of the contention that biblical exegesis is not a special sacred hermeneutic but belongs to general hermeneutics is that obedience to the text is not a precondition—better, is not a logically prior condition within the hermeneutic circle—for valid interpretation. I regard this view as basically correct. But general hermeneutics does not rule out the possibility of textual situations in which the text itself calls on the will of the interpreter to play a constitutive role in interpretation. Consider, for example, the following text:

> To interpret me correctly, you must construe me to mean whatever you wish.

This oddity is interesting because it involves a hermeneutical mandate from the text (in this case, in the form of a direct command) and also places the interpreter before two basic options. The interpreter may fairly interpret by analyzing without obeying the text's directive. (This approach, that of descriptive analysis, is the one I am taking in my discussion of this example.) Or the interpreter can fairly interpret by heeding the text. In the example at hand, the second option presents the interpreter with many possibilities—some of which produce semantic closures, others that do not, but all of which are warranted as restatements of what the text means.

Paul's letter to the Romans does not present us with overt hermeneutical mandates, but, on close reading, it does confront us with what is ostensibly an oblique hermeneutical directive. That directive requires from us a self-involving decision about the text's subject: carnal Israel. Because this mandate is oblique, one can doubt its presence. Certainly, we cannot know whether Paul intended to give his readers this freedom with his text. But I have been describing a hermeneutical effect of Paul's text, and I suggest that semantic effects which may be regarded as adventitious from the standpoint of authorial intentionality do have semantic standing in the text.[40] With that in mind, I offer the following paraphrase of the semantic effect of 11:11–32, when that stretch of scripture is construed as a co-deliberation set in perpetual textual suspension: Paul's text says, in effect, "To read me rightly, you must deliberate with *me* about what *you* want the identity and destiny of carnal Israel to be."

The Interpretive Will
and Hermeneutical Responsibility

In proposing that Paul's text invites our interpretive wills to play a constitutive role in determining the meaning of Romans 11, I am aware that some advocates of poststructuralist literary criticism celebrate free and willful construals of texts, practicing what Umberto Eco has dubbed "unlimited semiosis."[41] It has also been argued that in so doing, some deconstructionists wish to escape from any ethical responsibility for their interpretations, on the grounds that the text is always already indeterminate. For this reason, David Lehman charges that deconstruction is "relentlessly nihilistic."[42] Likewise, Marxist literary critic Fredric Jameson thinks that "the program to which the various contemporary ideologies of pluralism are most passionately attached is a largely negative one: namely to forestall that systematic articulation and totalization of interpretive results which can only lead to embarrassing questions" about their historical location and "the ultimate ground of narrative and textual production."[43]

But if one eschews the nihilism of (some forms of) deconstruction, then, by recognizing the role of the will in interpretation, one holds the interpreter partly responsible for the meaning of the text. Co-deliberation then requires the guidance of an ethic of interpretation. Hence we might expand the implicit hermeneutical directive of Romans 11 as follows:

> To read me rightly, you must deliberate with *me* about what *you* want the identity and destiny of carnal Israel to be. If you refuse to deliberate, you have not given me a fair hearing. If you accept, you become co-accountable for what my text means.

The question of the interpretive will and hermeneutical responsibility is often neglected in discussions of exegetical and theological method. While there may be a general acknowledgment that ideology, as reflective of some generalized will or interest,[44] plays a role in interpretation, relatively few discussions of hermeneutics accord a formal place to the will in hermeneutical method. A notable exception is Juan Luis Segundo's analysis of the relation between the hermeneutic circle and ideology.[45] Segundo quotes with approval the following words from Karl Mannheim's *Ideology and Utopia*: "An increasing number of concrete cases makes it evident that (a) every formulation of a problem is made possible only by a *previous actual human experience* which involves such a problem; (b) in selection from the multiplicity of data there is involved an *act of will* on the part of the knower; and (c) forces arising out of living experience are significant in *the direction which the treatment of the problem* follows."[46]

If there is no escaping "acts of will" in interpretation, then it is important to assign volition its proper place in hermeneutical method. Segundo formalizes volition as a constitutive moment in hermeneutics, assigning it a function analogous to that of "preunderstanding" in Rudolf Bultmann's hermeneutic.[47] Segundo does not suggest that an explicit precommitment might be—or should be—changed through encounter with the text. Commitments are shaped through life experience, and only life experience, defined broadly, can alter them.[48]

Life experience, however, is shaped by ideology, according to Segundo. Hence what Segundo describes is the ideological determination of interpretation: that is, ideology precedes commitment, and commitment governs the way in which one interprets the text. Having already expressed his own will to a revolutionary use of the Bible, Segundo therefore emphasizes that one cannot know in advance which ideology embodies the one, right revolutionary consciousness.[49] If one chooses self-consciously and critically at all, one must choose among competing ideologies, each of which claims to envision more accurately than its competitors how to make the world a more just and humane place. "There are an infinite number of more or less revolutionary processes in real-life praxis and choosing between them presupposes personal motivations and a conception of the overall process that stem from prior conditionings in the mind."[50] Thus, if some forms of deconstruction relieve authors and interpreters of moral responsibility for what they do with language, Segundo's hermeneutic makes the ethical moment decisive for interpretation. Segundo wants interpreters to make their ideological options explicit.

But if interpreters stand before various ideologies as options in a pluralistic world, can they distinguish the meanings of texts as objects from the ideologies of knowers as interpreters? Can a text speak against the ideology that informs the hermeneutical commitments of the interpreter? These questions can be treated from two angles. The first is the perspective of disagreement between interpreters. The second is the perspective of disagreement between interpreter and text.

It is certainly possible to give an ideological critique of an interpretation. When such a critique takes a prophetic form, where the text is applied in judgment on the exposed ideology of the interpreter, the claim is being made, at least implicitly, that the text can challenge ideology. But the text at odds with "my" interpretation is always someone else's interpretation— arguably, an interpretation in the grip of some other ideology. If one accepts that ideology always figures formatively in the interpretive process, then it might appear that interpretation can only reproduce ideology, and any debate about competing interpretations is never anything more than a contest among whatever fixed number of ideologies happen to be contending with one another "under the table."

But this view glosses over the difficulties that attend any effort to configure *plausible* interpretations of scripture for use in constructive theology and ethics. This brings us to the second angle of vision: the conflict between text and interpreter. The text may be somewhat malleable hermeneutically, owing to its semantic range, but it is not mere raw material for whatever symbolic universes a hermeneutic demiurge might want to fashion. Biblical texts are scarcely susceptible to any and all ideological constructions. The possibilities for persuasive theological argument from scripture are always limited in a given hermeneutical situation. The range of plausible interpretation has its disputed borders, but they are borders nonetheless. Moreover, interpreters often encounter these borders as clear barriers to their own interpretive will. Thus, when Robin Scroggs adapts the punch line of an old joke, "You can't get there from here," to epitomize the problem of applying New Testament ethics to contemporary Christian life, he is at least tacitly admitting that he cannot get what he wants from scripture (a relevant word on the contemporary issues he is discussing).[51] In so doing, he is also honoring the objectivity of the text.

Canonical Adjudication

If we are co-responsible for the meaning of Romans, what should we do with multiple plausible interpretations of the identity of Israel in Romans?

Answering this question depends on whether we regard Romans as a document of ancient Christianity or as part of Christian scripture. I have been treating Romans as a scriptural text. Now it is time to consider more precisely what that means.

We have many uses for texts. Some common examples are:

1. to understand the past by establishing and explaining "the way it really was"[52] (a historical-reconstructive use);
2. to learn what an ancient author or community sought to communicate in a text (a history-of-ideas use);
3. to make decisions based on a contractual relationship (a legal use);
4. to think through (and, in so doing, to make discoveries about) a subject matter (a dialogical use).

The methods appropriate to these uses overlap. But the different uses also require some differences of interpretive method.

For example, the second use requires an establishment of authorial intent through the probabilistic method of historical detective work, but authorial intent is not always decisive for the third use. It often happens that parties enter into a contractual relationship assuming different understandings of the wording of the instrument that is to express their joint intent. When a court is later called upon to settle a dispute arising from such a conflict of interpretation, it typically cannot use a purely intentionalist hermeneutic in deciding what the contract means. It must resort to other considerations, such as conventional linguistic usage, standards of reasonableness, and so forth. As E. Allan Farnsworth sums up this point in a standard text on contracts, one should "look with skepticism on the judicial

commonplace that in interpreting a contract the court merely carries out
'the intentions of the parties'."[53] Farnsworth continues:

> The court does indeed carry out their intentions in those relatively rare cases
> in which the parties attached the same meaning to the language in question.
> But if the parties attached different meanings to that language, the court's
> task is the more complex one of applying a standard of reasonableness to de-
> termine which party's intention is to be carried out at the expense of the
> other's. And if the parties attached no meaning to that language [or did not
> foresee its implications], its task is to find by a standard of reasonableness a
> meaning that does not accord with any intention at all.[54]

Now the *text* of a contract can have more than one use. A court will use
it one way; a biographer of one of the contracting parties will use it differently. Different uses of the "same" text may require different methods of
interpretation, and each method may require its own ethic of interpretation. While the rights of authors may be determinative in one use of texts,
in another use the operative rights may be those of readers.[55] In what follows, we will consider what method and what ethic of interpretation are
appropriate to interpreting the Bible as canon.

Canonical interpretation begins from the premise that scripture forms
a literary-theological integrity in which different parts of the canon exist
in a relationship of co-determination: one part affects the meaning of another part.[56] But there is a further aspect of canon as a genre. As Charles
Wood observes, "A canon is a canon only in use."[57] This suggests that the
use or purpose of scripture ought to bear on the interpretation of scripture.

One use of scripture has been aptly characterized by Gerald T. Sheppard, when he likens the Christian Bible to a "social contract between disparate groups of believers who share some degree of consensus and must
seek through the interpretation of scripture to justify how they will share,
in fact, the same Torah [or faith] in the future."[58] The identity of the
church is maintained by common appeal to the Bible, which is itself the
"contract" of that identity. Since a contract that establishes and maintains
a common identity is a covenant, we may conceive of scripture as a social
covenant between Christians. To the extent that Christians embrace this
covenant, they are obliged to make their case, through appeal to scripture,
for what they urge as the right faith and practice of the church.

If the Bible is a kind of Christian covenant, then a legal model may shed
light on the concept of canonicity. It is important to stress at the outset, however, that the use of such a model does not mean that we are to order the Bible
under the larger, generic rubric of law. The legal model is simply a metaphor
that draws attention to some neglected but illuminating similarities between
law and scripture. Both are normative texts, intended to guide the lives of
communities.[59] Thus the meaning of both legal and scriptural texts is finally

an applied sense. That sense must be construed from a range of reasonable interpretations, with consideration of their implications. In the words of jurist Richard Posner, "A choice among semantically plausible interpretations of a text, in circumstances remote from those contemplated by its drafters, requires the exercise of discretion and the weighing of consequences."[60] Hence we may think of canonical interpretation as an act of adjudication.

Canonical adjudication means resolving the indeterminate text through a specific set of hermeneutical moves carried out with a view to the use of the text as scripture. It may mean choosing one defensible construal over another or doing justice to reasonable opposing construals of the text through a higher-order synthesis, whether through a compromise or through a tensive dialectic that seeks to do justice to both. On this theory, there is no difference between doing justice to the text and doing justice to reasonable interpretations of the text, since the latter are themselves statements of the text's apparent meanings.

In law, the practical or use-oriented aspect of interpretation is very old. Textual ambiguity gives rise to legitimate conflicts in interpretation, which must be resolved when they reach litigation. The Greek and Latin rhetoricians recognized this. When faced with ambiguity in a legal text, Quintilian says, "the only questions which confront us will be, sometimes which of the two interpretations is most natural, and always which of the two interpretations is most equitable, and what was the intention of the person who wrote or uttered the words" (*Institutio Oratoria* 7.9.15).[61] It follows that if one cannot prove which of two interpretations is most natural linguistically, and if there is no possibility of adducing from some other source the intention of the one who wrote or uttered the words in question, then the interpretation of a legal text *as a meaning to be applied* must be established by the principle of equity alone.

I propose that we look to the Christian canon itself for substantial principles to guide canonical adjudication. Among these are canonical indicators of the aim and focus, or *scopus*, of scripture.[62] I offer my own working definition of the focal aim of scripture, presenting it as a kind of hermeneutical stipulation in preparation for the discussions to follow.

In the first book of the New Testament, the canonical Jesus pronounces on the fundamental meaning and purpose of scripture. In an encounter with a professional interpreter who seeks to test him with the question "What is the greatest commandment in the law?" Jesus answers as follows:

> You shall love the Lord your God with all your heart, and with all your soul, and with all your mind. This is the greatest and first commandment. And a second is like it, You shall love your neighbor as yourself. On these two commandments hang all the law and the prophets.
>
> (Matt. 22:37–40)

Although parallels to this passage appear in Mark and Luke, it is only in Matthew that the double commandment is presented as the basis of scripture as a whole. These two commandments together establish the purpose of scripture, consideration of which ought to guide all interpretation of scripture.[63] The fact that Jesus, having satisfied the lawyer's request by identifying "the great and first commandment," goes on to add a second commandment suggests that the first commandment cannot function hermeneutically without the second. Moreover, in Matt. 7:12, Jesus says, "In everything do to others as you would have them do to you; for this is the law and the prophets." This suggests that the second commandment *can* stand on its own as a summary of scripture. While the first commandment may be greater in the hierarchy of obligations, the second commandment appears to include the first and to carry hermeneutical priority.[64] The commandment to love one's neighbor gives decisive guidance for understanding the commandment to love God. For those who would be loyal to God in all things, including the interpretation of scripture, the second great commandment is the primary criterion for the adjudication of scripture.

In a very appealing formulation, Paul Lehmann has described God's activity in the world as an effort to "make and keep human life human."[65] Scripture's self-purpose, as expressed by Jesus in Matthew 22, justifies this epitome of the divine purpose in history. As an instrument of that purpose, the aim of scripture is to promote a love of God that expresses itself in love for one's neighbor. Love for neighbor, in turn, requires a humane and humanizing practice toward others, including one's enemies. But I argue further that this humane practice of love for neighbor has hermeneutical implications. In expressing the aim, or *scopus*, of scripture, love of neighbor supplies a constructive principle of interpretive adjudication. One might say, then, that it belongs to the purpose of scripture to make and keep the church's life "humane," which means that canonical adjudication ought to be guided by principles of love and humanity.

Christians, of course, differ in their understandings of what love of neighbor means. One learns not only from scripture but also from many other sources, including history and personal experience, what love is and what it requires. In commanding love, Jesus himself assumes that his hearers know or can learn what it means to love genuinely and fully. To take a paradigmatic example, they must already know what love is and that love is the purpose of scripture in order to see that "the sabbath was made for humankind, and not humankind for the sabbath" (Mark 2:27). Paul, too, often assumes that his hearers—even those not schooled in the scriptures—know or can learn what love means, even apart from consulting scripture. That is certainly his assumption in Romans and Galatians, when he commands love as the fulfilling of the law but does not command his audience to study the scriptures in order to find out what love is. Thus, New Testament writers often use but do not define the concept of "love" and other similar ethical principles, taking for granted that their readers have adequate notions of these ideas. The New Testament writers typically rely on common, public understandings of what is good and righteous.[66]

To understand what the scriptures intend, we must know certain things about love. We also learn what love is from scripture. But scripture *by itself* cannot mediate that knowledge. We judge what love is and what it requires by drawing on personal experience and by reflecting on what others have to say about it as we study scripture in community. Therefore, defining and using the focal aim of scripture is a moral task that assumes experiential knowledge and entails ethical debate in which we adjudicate between plausible interpretations of scripture by contending for particular conceptions of what love demands.[67]

3

Prophetic Paul

In an 1895 address, E. F. Ströter (1846–1922) offered a series of explanations to his Christian audience of why Jews reject Jesus as the messiah. The messiah, Ströter observed, was to bring universal peace, but Jesus did not usher in that peace. Not only that, but "fifteen centuries of Christian history during which the professed followers of Jesus have shed more Jewish blood alone than Titus and Epiphanes combined, accentuate the Jew's objection."[1] In the same context, Ströter also quoted the following words from the *Reformer and Jewish Times* (December 6, 1877):

> The Jews reject the belief in Jesus as the Messiah because his coming did not fulfill the prophecies of the Bible in regard to the real Messiah; because these prophecies have not since been fulfilled; because, of the important events that were to accompany the coming of the Messiah, not one has come to pass. . . . When these prophecies are fulfilled the Jews will believe that the Messiah has come.

Or as Franz Rosenzweig wrote in 1918, in a letter to his Christian friend Hans Ehrenberg, "We shall see whether or not Jesus was the Messiah when—the Messiah arrives."[2] Then there are Martin Buber's words, now well known to Jewish and Christian theologians, about the difference between Jews and Christians:

> To the Christian the Jew is the stubborn fellow who in an unredeemed world is still waiting for the Messiah. For the Jew the Christian is a heedless fellow who in an unredeemed world affirms that somehow or other redemption has taken place.[3]

Dispensationalism, the tradition with which Ströter identified, has long been emphatic in agreeing with the protest of "stubborn" Jews against Christian spiritualization of the Jewish scriptures, by which the church has arrogated to itself the identity and destiny of Israel and claimed that Christ has brought the redemption promised to Israel. But with the exception of the Dispensationalists, it was not until the post-Holocaust era that Christian theologians began to consider that the Christian hope of the kingdom of God might be misconceived apart from Christian confession that the Jewish people are true Israel.

The post-Holocaust era also brought a heightened awareness among Christians of how deep anti-Jewishness runs in Christianity. Rosemary Radford Ruether brought this point home in a 1968 article titled "Theological Anti-Semitism in the New Testament."[4] Ruether criticized Christianity for a double move against Judaism, which she called a "historicizing of the eschatological" on the one hand and a "spiritualizing of the eschatological" on the other.[5] The spiritualizing hermeneutic rejects the historical literalism of Jewish eschatology as carnal but discovers a spiritual meaning in the Jewish scriptures that discloses the church's own being and destiny as otherworldly. In this theological scheme, the church's temporal supersession of Judaism signifies a supersession of merely earthly or historical salvation, of which the negated Jewish past, with its carnal messianic hopes, becomes the enduring sign.

Much so-called mainline Christian theology has done an about-face over the last thirty years. Today, many non-Dispensationalists affirm that the Jewish people are true Israel. This affirmation has, in turn, brought about a rethinking of the symbol "carnal Israel." For some, Christian *affirmation* of carnal Israel involves not only a renunciation of anti-Semitism but also openness to interreligious dialogue without the presumption of Christian superiority.[6] At the same time, affirming carnal Israel represents disavowal of Christian otherworldliness. Thus, for some Christians, carnal Israel has become a sign of a good kind of this-worldliness—of hope for history, respect for the blessings of creation, and a renewed commitment to social responsibility.

This chapter and the next explore whether there is any basis in Paul for these or other such typological reinterpretations of the identity and vocation of Israel in Christian theology.

J. Christiaan Beker: The Sign of Israel in Apocalyptic Paul

Of special significance for Christian rethinking of Paul's teaching about Israel and the relevance of that teaching for contemporary Christian theology is J. Christiaan Beker's study *Paul's Apocalyptic Gospel: The Coming Triumph of God.*[7] Although Paul's teaching about Israel is not a central focus of Beker's book, I propose that it plays a constitutive role at the implicit hermeneutical level of Beker's appropriation of Paul. Moreover, since Dispensationalism makes the question of distinguishing the church from (true) Israel a hermeneutical key for its reading of the Bible, I follow up my discussion of Beker by examining a Dispensationalist reading of Israel in Paul. This should prove especially interesting because Beker himself chooses a Dispensationalist as one of his partners in dialogue.

In *Paul's Apocalyptic Gospel*, Beker seeks to show that Paul's apocalyptic vision holds abiding relevance for today's church, calling Christians to practice an activist social ethic inspired by hope for God's final salvation of the whole creation.[8] In what follows, I analyze the hermeneutic that generates this conclusion. I argue that although Beker insists on the apocalyptic unsurpassability of the core of Paul's gospel, he in fact uses a typological rather than an apocalyptic hermeneutic in appropriating Paul. The Pauline theme of God's faithfulness to the promises made to Israel plays a crucial hermeneutical role in that typological appropriation.

But before proceeding, I wish to make three things clear. First, mine is an appreciative critique. I find Beker's vision of Paul's relevance for today largely attractive. Second, "apocalyptic" is a slippery category. Beker uses the word primarily to accent the way in which Paul's gospel embraces the whole cosmic order as the creation that God intends to save. I use the term primarily as a hermeneutical category. Nevertheless, because Beker asserts the apocalyptic claim of Paul's gospel in its *literal* intent and argues that the apocalyptic core of Paul's gospel is betrayed if this literal intent is not honored, there is a fundamental hermeneutical assumption in Beker's use of the term as well. Third, because Beker does not fully explain his method for appropriating Paul, I have been forced at many points to read between the lines and reconstruct what appears to be the implicit hermeneutic logic of Beker's theological moves.

Beker's stated hermeneutic is as follows: "Paul's apocalyptic gospel is not to be defended on biblicist grounds; rather it has a *catalytic* power for the church today."[9] Activating this "catalytic function" means differentiating the abiding core of Pauline apocalyptic from its contingent application and drawing out implications for our time directly from that core.[10] The core of Pauline apocalyptic includes (1) the vindication of the God of Israel; (2) universalism (a gospel embracing the whole of creation); (3) modified dualism; and (4) imminence.[11]

One example of drawing implications from the abiding core, rather than from Paul's contingent applications, is Beker's treatment of Paul's expectation of an imminent end of history. The nonoccurrence of the imminent appearance of the cosmic Christ looks like a decisive disconfirmation of the "literal intent" of Paul's gospel and grounds for some kind of demythologizing of Paul's apocalyptic hope. To forestall this conclusion, Beker makes two hermeneutical moves. One is to deny that imminence is an essential feature of Paul's apocalyptic gospel.[12] The other is to interpret the real meaning of imminence as urgency, a passion for the redemption of creation. We will examine each of these moves in turn.

While it is true that Paul does not dwell on the imminence of Christ's return, much less set out a timetable, imminence is not so easily separated from the apocalyptic core. Paul announces an inaugurated eschatology, whose apocalyptic consummation is not simply a future expectation but a process already underway. The Pauline metaphor of "first fruits" (Rom. 8:23; 1 Cor. 15:20), for example—like the agricultural metaphors used in the Synoptics to describe the kingdom's arrival—expresses an organic conception that, by its very logic, must be fulfilled within the generation of Jesus and Paul.[13]

In interpreting imminence as urgency, it appears that Beker substitutes a psychological corollary of Paul's core apocalyptic theology for a disconfirmed element of that core.[14] Or one could view Beker's approach as a typological reappropriation: Paul's urgent expectation of an imminent manifestation of the new creation is a type of the hope we ought to have under very different assumptions about the course of history and the form of its future salvation. Typological interpretation discovers (in history or experience) or projects (for the future) an analogous correlation rather than an identity between type and antitype. Hence between type and antitype are both likeness and dissimilarity. In the example at hand, urgent expectation of a literal cosmic transformation is the point of likeness; literal imminence is a dissimilarity that drops out. It seems, then, that the "catalytic" function of Pauline apocalyptic entails typological appropriation of the literal core.

In Beker's use of Paul's vision of cosmic salvation there also appears an implicitly typological reinterpretation. While the *literal intent* of apocalyptic is to be preserved (that intent being literal cosmic transformation), the particularity of the mythical apocalyptic imagery is not transferable to our time.[15] But since Paul himself surely equated the literal meaning of his apocalyptic language with its intent, Beker's distinction between the mythic garb of the imagery and the literal intent in effect typologizes that imagery. Paul's image of the future redemption becomes a type of a future but unspecified form of cosmic transformation, which might be fulfilled in ways quite different from any Paul could have imagined.

A central aim of Beker's effort to reassert this apocalyptic hope for modern Christian faith is to establish a basis in Paul for an activist Christian social ethic. Here, too, Beker draws implications from the core rather than from Paul's contingent applications. According to Beker, Paul "did not always develop and clarify the practical consequences of his own theological insights, as for instance in his stance toward the state or in his assessment of the *cultural* implications of his *ecclesial* insistence on the removal of racial, sexual, cultural, and economic distinctions (Rom. 13:1–7; Gal 3:28)."[16] But we can advocate a social ethic of radical egalitarianism as an implication of Paul's apocalyptic hope, which "compels an ethic that strains and labors to move God's creation toward that future triumph of God promised in Jesus Christ and to which the presence of the Spirit propels us."[17] Nevertheless, even if Paul advocated a radically egalitarian ecclesiology as a present expression of the coming apocalyptic social transformation, there are also impediments in the apocalyptic core itself to developing an activist Christian ethic aimed at making society more like the ideal of an egalitarian church. For example, while Christians are called to "work for the good of all" (Gal. 6:10), Paul never urges Christians to work for the common good with those outside the church. Yet it is just such a partnership that is required to keep an activist Pauline social ethic from degenerating into Christian triumphalism. Beker knows this, and therefore he insists that since the apocalyptic hope encompasses the whole created order, Christians are to recognize that their neighbors in the world "are persons who not only need us but whom we need as well."[18] "And we need them," Beker says, "in several ways":

> First, they clarify the meaning of our life for us and compel us to break out of our various Christian ghettos. Second, they remind us that God's triumph will not take place without the participation of our "neighbors" in it, and so our "neighbors" compel us to struggle together with them for the liberation of all God's world. Third, and above all, once a person in the world is transformed into "my neighbor," we practice the manner of Paul's apocalyptic gospel, that is, we travel the way of the cross as the way in which God intends to bring about his kingdom.[19]

The difficulty with this interpretation is that Paul's core apocalyptic gospel does not seem to teach or assume that the church "needs" its neighbors in the ways Beker suggests. Paul's apocalyptic ecclesiology casts the church as the exclusive locus of God's saving presence and community-forming power in the world. Paul assumes that God's righteousness is a new creation formed in the Christian communities, where people are guided and empowered by the Spirit (2 Cor. 5:17; Gal. 6:14–15). Paul's explicit statements about humanity apart from Christ (e.g., Rom. 1:18–3:20), together with the logic of apocalyptic itself, suggest that the church's worldly neighbors are, in his view, unfit partners for "establishing signs and beachheads of the kingdom in our world."[20] In Paul's understanding, human beings outside the church suppress what truth of God's righteousness is available to them and lack the moral power to live out righteousness. Sin, as a cosmic power, has distorted their knowledge of God, perverted their sense of righteousness, and rendered them incapable of doing even the good that they may perceive and affirm (Rom. 1:18–32; 3:9–20; 7:7–24). Those living according to the flesh are scarcely suitable coworkers for a church guided and empowered by the Spirit (Rom. 8:1–8; Gal.

5:16–25). The "need" would appear to be in only one direction—the world's need for Christ and his church. This is why the church, when it has been culturally and politically empowered, has found it so easy to carry out an imperialistic mission toward the world in the name of the universal Pauline gospel. Christians are called to practice the good *toward* the world, not *with* the world in a shared praxis.

Although Beker insists on the inviolability of the literal apocalyptic core of Paul's gospel, it appears that, in the example at hand, he appropriates part of that core typologically. In Beker's reading of Paul, it is as if the apocalyptic "body," which is the church, becomes a sign of the world, as a body in which Christians are interdependently related with non-Christians in the same ways that the members of the body are said to be interdependent in 1 Corinthians 12. Despite the fact that Paul restricts all present spiritual goods and powers to the elect community, Beker's appropriation lets the world stand where the church belongs in the apocalyptic symbol system, so that the light and the labor of God's kingdom become the shared gift and task of all people.

Other features of Beker's discussion reinforce the impression that Beker uses a typological hermeneutic to reinterpret the core of Paul's apocalyptic gospel. Summarizing the demise of apocalyptic in subsequent Christian generations, Beker makes two initial observations that appear to be causally linked in his mind. First, "the surrender of apocalyptic thought forms produced an alienation of Christianity from its original Jewish matrix, with the result that the messianic expectations of Judaism—evoked by God's promises to Israel—were diverted into non-apocalyptic Christology." Second, this surrender "produced a spiritualistic interpretation of the gospel."[21] For Beker, it is evidently Paul's affirmation of carnal Israel's election and hopes—an affirmation preserved in the course of Paul's universalizing modification of the Jewish hope—that keeps the new creation oriented to present history and social structures.[22] Thus, Beker construes Paul's affirmation of the literal identity and destiny of Israel as signifying Paul's concern for the concrete this-worldliness of the gospel hope. If I read Beker rightly, he is suggesting that Pauline apocalyptic universalizes this concreteness, so that the this-worldly promises are not limited to the nation of Israel but belong to all human beings. It appears that Israel's history and promissory hope provide typological patterns that Paul universalizes (without spiritualizing).

Likewise, Beker's description of the church's social witness appears to be modeled on the social ethic of the Israelite prophets. At least this typological reading of Israel would explain the social ethic Beker draws from Paul, where the church's "neighbors" are not simply objects of Christian mission but partners in building God's kingdom. *Israel is a type of the church and the church is a type of the world.* Both the concrete this-worldly hope of

Israel and the social ethic of Israel are transferred to the church, and thus, through the universalizing effect of Pauline apocalyptic, both that hope and that ethic are transferred to the world as the church's present partners in hope and social responsibility.

If my reading of Beker is correct, Beker's insistence on the unsurpassable letter of the apocalyptic center of Paul's gospel conflicts with his own implicitly typologizing appropriations of that core. Beker's interest in a gospel that is an adequate answer to the scope of human suffering and cosmic disorder leads him to stress the unsurpassability of the apocalyptic hope. His concern to ground a relevant social ethic in Paul's gospel leads him to adopt a typological hermeneutic in which the theme of carnal Israel has a critical mediating function. But where are the warrants in the historical Paul for a typological interpretation of Paul's own apocalyptic theology? Paul reads the Jewish scriptures typologically, but he presents his own gospel in the garb of apocalyptic finality. We will return to this question after we have examined Paul's teaching about Israel through the lens of a biblical scholar who affirms the Jewish people's enduring identity as true Israel and rejects any typological appropriation by the church of Israel's identity, vocation, and hope.

E. F. Ströter: Elect Judaism in Dispensationalist Paul

In working out his apocalyptic reading of Paul, Beker distances himself from the sensationalist neoapocalypticism represented by Hal Lindsey's best-selling book *The Late Great Planet Earth*.[23] But the theological tradition that Lindsey crassly exploits also boasts able and humane scholars. One of them is E. F. Ströter.

Ströter and the formative Dispensationalism in which he worked present an interesting perspective on the question broached in the first part of this chapter. By rejecting a hermeneutic that justifies blanket Christian appropriation and spiritualization of the Old Testament covenants made by God with the Jewish people, Dispensationalism in effect affirms a kind of hermeneutical reciprocity between the Testaments. While the exegetical conclusions adduced to support the larger Dispensationalist theological system are often forced, the effort to do justice to the Jewish scriptures on their own terms, within a Christian biblical theology, is notable. Especially significant is the fact that Ströter's book *Die Judenfrage und ihre göttliche Lösung nach Römer 11*[24] influenced Karl Barth's radical rethinking of the church and Israel[25] and thus contributed to the Barthian turn that inaugurated a new, post-Holocaust Christian theology of Israel among students of Barth, such as Paul van Buren and Jürgen Moltmann.[26] Moreover, Ströter's studies of Paul anticipate much of the new view of Israel in Paul that one meets in contemporary Pauline scholarship.[27]

As inerrantists,[28] Dispensationalists disallow the possibility of any theological contradictions in the Bible, which leads them to distort, among other things, the canonical representation of biblical prophecy. Nevertheless, something remains to be learned from how a Dispensationalist such as Ströter reads the canonical Paul. This is especially true when it comes to Paul's teaching about Israel. Of particular interest is how Ströter treats (1) what he takes to be Paul's assumption that the promises of God to Israel have a this-worldly "literal" meaning and (2) what he construes as Paul's affirmation (in Rom. 11:25–29) that these promises are irrevocable. On these two points Beker and Ströter are in basic exegetical agreement. But while Beker sees Paul's refusal to apply, without remainder, the scriptural promises to fleshly Israel as proof that Paul's apocalyptic gospel has a social-prophetic aspect that the church is called to actualize, Ströter is more concerned with the bearing of these promises on fleshly Israel itself, which includes for him the question of Israel's practice of its own vocation.

Against Christianity's conceit that it alone has a divine mission to the world, Ströter insists that Israel retains its vocation to bring the light of the Torah to humanity. Rejecting the Christian presumption that there is only a Christian mission *to* Israel, and not a mission *of* Israel to the rest of the world,[29] Ströter asserts that the Jewish people "have remained and will remain for all coming ages the exclusive bearers of the whole divine mediation of salvation to humanity."[30] It is Christian arrogance that leads the church to deny what Paul teaches in Romans. To protect its self-superiority, the church suppresses the scriptural teaching about the Jewish people, discarding Romans 11 as "oriental fantasy"[31] or reinterpreting it spiritually so as to maintain the church's place at the center of theology, salvation, and history.

According to Ströter, the divine promises to Israel are that Israel would persist throughout history as a nation, or "people"; that Israel would possess the land (Abrahamic covenant); and that Israel, under the messiah's reign, would mediate the salvation of the kingdom of God to the world (Davidic covenant) through the law as an instrument of social justice (Mosaic covenant).[32] Christendom spiritualizes and expropriates these promises for itself, but Paul teaches that the church is not to be the agent of this millennial mission or a mediator in the reunion of the messiah Jesus with the synagogue. According to Ströter, Jewish Zionism (a fledgling movement when Ströter wrote) gets closer to the core of this Pauline truth.[33]

If not only the "gifts" of God, which include election, are irrevocable but also the divine "calling," how does that call remain Israel's now that the messiah has come? Ströter plausibly takes "calling" (κλῆσις) in 11:29 as including the idea of a divinely appointed *vocation*. He also construes the future salvation of Israel as a vindication, before the world and the church, of Israel's claim to have a nonrescindable call from God. He therefore assumes, in line with the Dispensationalist tradition to which he belongs, that God will confirm Israel's vocation when the Deliverer comes. This means that Israel will fulfill its vocation to the world and be recognized by the world for this special work. Ströter further assumes that Paul is writing within the larger scheme of scripture and hence that Paul takes for granted the this-worldly hope of the millennium, when God will establish a worldwide theocracy (according to the Dispensationalist reading of the Bible). Moreover, in the millennium Israel will fulfill the vocation to which Paul refers in 11:29 (cf. 9:4), when Israel completes its vocation to teach the world about God's righteousness, grace, and mercy.[34] In the meantime, the Jewish people must maintain their distinct identity as God's covenant people by practicing traditional Judaism.[35]

The idea that Israel has an obligation to maintain its Jewish identity through keeping the law may never have occurred to the historical Paul. Paul envisions the impending salvation of all Israel in his own time. He therefore has no need to concern himself with the question of how Israel is to remain Israel, as God's covenant people, for generations (while the fullness of the gentiles "comes in"). But Ströter takes for granted that scripture, in speaking of Israel, is wise to the fact that generations of Jews would come and go between the time of Paul and the time of Israel's future salvation. Hence, Ströter contends that God never rescinds the charge to the Jewish people that they keep the law. Their vocation is to guard this law and share its light with the world.[36] Even Christian Jews fall under this divine mandate to keep the law. Thus the Pauline gospel affirms the practice of Judaism by non-Christian Jews, and not only for the narrow purpose of preserving their ethnic identity as the objects of God's covenantal mercy. Practicing Judaism is a matter of maintaining their religious identity and vocation as God's people.

This would suggest that, for Ströter, Jewish faithfulness to the law in the present age is a divine vocation. This does not mean that Israel is now fulfilling its mission to the world, only that it has such a mission and rightly guards the Torah through history, even though it wrongly keeps the light of that Torah from the nations.[37] It is true that, under this view, a present mission of Israel to the world is not really possible, owing to God's hardening of Israel. But Ströter mitigates his critique of the synagogue by making a much sharper critique of the church and Christendom. In the Dispensationalist theology of history, each covenant people deteriorates morally and spiritually until its age draws to a close. In Ströter's conception, the Jewish people reached the nadir of their spiritual degradation during the time of Jesus. Since then, it has not been Jews but Christians who have become the sign, for this age, of humanity's moral and spiritual corruption. It is characteristic of the church's degraded spiritual condition, Ströter maintains, that Christians have been unwilling to face up to their own degenerate moral state. Instead, they have concentrated on developing a minute critique of the Jews.[38]

Adopting the language of Jesus' parable in Luke 18:9–14, Ströter describes the church as the self-righteous Pharisee who scorns "the poor Jewish tax collector."[39] But Christians cannot imagine such a reversal of roles. "That Christians and Jews exchange roles, that Christians could become the Pharisees and Jews could really become the humble tax collectors, who will go down to their house and land justified—self-satisfied Christianity would never dream of that."[40] This allegory blends what Ströter has been describing as a *present* role reversal with his expectation of the future millennial justification of the Jewish people. This is a further indication that, for Ströter, the present "hardening" of Israel does not mean that Christians must devalue the spiritual and moral life of Jews, as if Christians were theologically required to interpret Jewish ethical-religious practice as false or perverted.

It is clear that for Ströter, a Paul who assumes that the Jewish people remain God's people Israel after the appearance of Christ—possessing their own irrevocable gifts and calling from God, generation after generation—also presumes and *affirms*, by that assumption, not only God's preservation of the Jews but Judaism itself, by which Jews are constituted as true Israel.[41] Christians have traditionally thought that Israel's "blindness" is manifest in the fact that it continues to practice Judaism despite the appearance of Christ. But in Ströter's interpretation, Paul teaches that Israel is called by God to guard and practice the Torah generation after generation until the end of history. Hence to regard "Judaism" as a false or superseded religion is contradictory.

The upshot of Ströter's interpretation is the appearance of a double bind in the canonical Paul. Israel is accountable for its "no" to the messiah; at the same time, Jews must maintain their identity as Israel by practicing Judaism, which means that they ought not convert to Christianity. It would appear that after Judaism and Christianity emerged as distinct religions, which is an assumption of the Christian *canon* (but probably not of the historical Paul), Jewish faithfulness to God requires at least some version of the Jewish no to the Christian Jesus. Ströter avoids this interpretation because his hermeneutic has no place for dialectical theological construction. As a Dispensationalist, Ströter is attuned to the heterogeneity of the scriptural covenants, but he cannot conceive a Jewish no to Jesus Christ counting as an expression of faithfulness to the God of both Jews and Christians.

Nor does Ströter conceive of carnal Israel in the scriptures as a type for the church to imitate. The biblical church and the biblical Israel have not only distinct identities but also distinct vocations. There is something very appealing in Ströter's refusal to expropriate the identity and calling of Israel for the church. But it comes at the expense of making the church an otherworldly people, with thoroughly otherworldly tasks.

Prophetic Paul

It would be intriguing to see what a Dispensationalist such as Ströter would do with the implicitly typologizing hermeneutic that I have attributed to Beker. Beker's hermeneutic, I suggested, typologizes without spiritualizing; in this way, Beker seeks to honor the "letter" of Paul's apocalyptic gospel. But we noted that it is difficult to find a warrant in apocalyptic Paul for a typologizing appropriation of Paul. Paul reads the Jewish scriptures typologically, but he presents his own gospel with apocalyptic finality. Nevertheless, this finality or unsurpassability acquires a different cast in the canonical Paul. To see how the canon refracts Pauline apocalyptic, we begin by returning to Wayne Meeks's and Richard Hays's studies of Paul's uses of scripture in Romans 9—11.

According to Meeks, although Paul engages in considerable spiritual exegesis of the Jewish scriptures in Romans 9—11, he also affirms the literal sense of those scriptures.[42] Having applied the identity and destiny of Israel to gentiles, Paul goes on to honor the literal scriptural meaning of Israel's hope. On this interpretation, Paul does transfer the identity of Israel to the church, but not in a way that disinherits the Jewish people.

Richard Hays makes a related point when he argues that not only does Paul interpret scripture texts with sensitivity to their original contexts, but scripture itself also speaks through Paul, shaping the meaning of Romans beyond Paul's own awareness: "Scripture broods over this letter, calls Paul to account, speaks through him."[43] What Hays means is illustrated by his comments about Paul's use of Isa. 52:5 in Rom. 2:24. The rhetorical structure of Romans, Hays suggests, "lures the reader into expecting Israel's final condemnation" only to undermine that expectation in the later chapters.[44] Those who know scripture well discover that already in Romans 2, Paul's pronouncement of Israel's condemnation is qualified by the presence of an echo of hope for Israel from the scriptural context of Isa. 52:5.[45] If we accept the thesis that scripture quotations and allusions in Paul have a constitutive function in constructing the sense of Romans, then we must understand those scripture uses more deeply in relation to their original scriptural contexts. To interpret Paul rightly, Hays argues, we must pay attention to how the literal sense of Paul's Bible is at work in his letters to generate not only those meanings he intended but also meanings beyond his intentions.[46] Paul becomes Paul-with-his-canon, an intertextual field. What happens, then, when Paul-with-his-canon becomes part of a Christian Bible: Paul-with-his-canon *in* the canon?

Paul-with-His-Canon
in *the Canon*

Let us agree (1) that the logic of Rom. 11:25–29 honors the literal sense of scripture and (2) that scripture does generate meanings in Paul's text beyond his intentions. If we transfer these two ideas to the orbit of canonical interpretation, some momentous implications result. The use of an intertextual approach in canonical interpretation of Paul means constituting the object of theological interpretation as Paul-with-his-canon *in* the canon: that is, at the canonical level, the *inter*textual (the semantic relation between the Jewish scriptures and the Pauline letter) becomes the *intra*textual (the Pauline letter now forming part of a Christian Bible that includes the Jewish scriptures). Intertextual interpretation reveals an implied author (Paul) whose regard for the literal sense of scripture constrains him to honor that sense, even at the price of producing unresolved tensions with his typological uses of scripture. Canonical interpretation must correlate this Pauline affirmation of the literal sense of the scriptures with the intratextual presence of those very scriptures, along with Paul, in the Christian Bible.

Paul's use of these scriptures is a warrant in the New Testament for attributing authority to the literal sense of the Old Testament. And because Paul interprets typologically but also honors the literal sense, his witness to the authority of the literal reading of the Old Testament does not simply contradict the thoroughgoing typological reading of the Old Testament found elsewhere in the New Testament. Rather, it provides a hermeneutical model in the New Testament for treating the words of scripture as both literal signs and figurative types.

In addition, the Pauline hermeneutical dialectic of typological and literal readings provides a warrant in Paul for *construing his letters typologically in the light of the literal sense of the Old Testament.* That is, Paul's use of scripture doubles back on the *canonical* Paul, warranting the use of Paul's dialectical hermeneutic in reading both Paul and the Old Testament. That double hermeneutic would entail the sort of typological reading of the Old Testament that has often been justified in the name of Paul (and other New Testament writers), but it would also require a counterreading, in which Paul himself became a type to be interpreted in the light of the Old Testament. Thus the canonical Paul justifies a dialectical conception of the hermeneutical relationship between the Testaments. The Old Testament is to be read in the light of the New Testament, but the New Testament is also to be read *hermeneutically* in the light of the Old. If this hermeneutical dialectic is a balanced one, that ought to mean reading the New Testament *typologically* in the light of the Old, rather than only reading the Old Testament typologically in the light of the New.

At this point, it is useful to pause to distinguish between several meanings of the literal sense:

1. Letter as "law" (in Christian hermeneutics) versus the Spirit (and the gospel), a dichotomy that is sometimes joined with one of the other senses below.

2. The letter of the law (what stands written) versus the pur-
    pose or spirit of the law (its underlying concern or point),
    a basis for making distinctions that the ancient rhetori-
    cians called στάσις κατὰ ῥητὸν καὶ διάνοιαν.[47]
3. The original or primary sense of scripture as distinct
    from its typological applications.
4. The literal as the earthly/material (social, historical, etc.)
    versus the otherworldly/spiritual.

Our interest here is with meanings 3 and 4, not with the letter as a dead or
legalistic sense.

Hans Frei has made an astute observation about the literal sense in Christian hermeneutics. Speaking of what I have termed the third meaning of the
literal sense, Frei observes that from the beginning of Christian interpretation of scripture, the literal sense of the Jesus story was identical with its true
and *spiritual* sense, while the literal sense of the Jewish scriptures, expropri-
ated by Christians as the Old Testament, had to be accommodated to this
primary literal sense.[48] Following Meeks, we have found evidence that Paul
regards the literal sense of the Old Testament as a true and spiritual sense,
which Paul himself is bound to honor. Moreover, as I have argued, the historical Paul's affirmation of the letter of his scriptures folds back on the
canonical Paul, subordinating him, on one side of the resultant dialectic, to
the literal sense of the Old Testament and thus justifying a typological reading of his letters in the light of that literal sense: interpreting Paul typologically according to the literal sense of the Old Testament.

A typological interpretation of Paul according to the plain sense of his
scriptures would, among other things, require hermeneutical reciprocity
in the treatment of the church and Israel. Since Paul's own typological
readings involve exchanging carnal Israel in scripture for the church, we
are justified in using the Old Testament as a hermeneutical guide for construing the church in Romans as a type pointing beyond itself to a fulfillment in carnal Israel. By this I mean that, in their likeness in Paul, neither
the church nor Israel is a sign that hermeneutically supersedes the other;
they are co-determining signs. Just as Israel is a type of what Paul commands us to believe and hope about the church, so the church is a type of
what the Old Testament commands us to believe and hope about Israel. I
propose that this double-directional form of typological interpretation
provides a reasonable way to honor Paul's affirmation that the letter of the
scripture still stands, and to do so by taking into account that Paul's letters
belong to a Christian Bible in which the Jewish scriptures are part of the
literary canonical context in which his authorship is found.

It would appear, however, that there is a significant obstacle to *recipro-
cal* typological interpretation between the Testaments. It is impossible to

carry out a typological interpretation of Paul, using the Old Testament as literal standard, and still uphold the eschatological meaning of Christ's life, death, and resurrection and the constitution of the church through the Spirit. To make the story of the eschaton[49] a type in a series that takes its cue from the Old Testament story of Israel would contradict the meaning of eschaton. The eschaton is, by definition, absolute and unsurpassable, which makes it intractable to typological use.

The Conversion of Apocalyptic into Prophecy: A Canonical Effect

Beker's appreciation for the apocalyptic character of the historical Paul's gospel leads him into a hermeneutical difficulty. The apocalyptic core presents itself as unsurpassable, but Beker wants to appropriate it using a dialogical hermeneutic that includes some degree of typological reinterpretation. Clearly, the warrant for using such a hermeneutic on Paul cannot come from the historical Paul himself. But the conversion of the historical Paul into the canonical Paul has an effect that does warrant typological reinterpretation of Paul. I characterize this effect as the conversion of apocalyptic Paul into prophetic Paul.

In Beker's usage of the term "apocalyptic" the emphasis falls on the global scope of redemption, with the result that Pauline apocalyptic comes to signify a universal and cosmic expansion of concrete "prophetic" hope. As we have seen, in Beker's understanding, this apocalyptic expansion—hope for the entire created order—both includes and outstrips hermeneutically the literal language of prophetic hope. But there is another way in which "prophetic" and "apocalyptic" can be contrasted. As I have suggested, apocalyptic represents itself as final revelation. By contrast, it is common to think of prophetic revelation as inherently provisional. In this usage of terms, prophecy and apocalyptic stand for two different ways of conceiving God's relation to history. The assumptions of prophecy put all of history, including prophetic announcements, under the aspect of contingency, while apocalyptic regards history under the aspect of otherworldly determinism, treating its own disclosures as revelations of what God has foreordained and therefore of what must be. Most important, apocalyptic represents a form of knowledge that excludes the possibility of its own surpassability and recuperation through some future reappropriation under new circumstances. In an apocalyptic scheme of history, not only the shape of the End and the eschaton but also the course of history before the End are fixed. Where prophecy announces possibilities, an apocalypse discloses the unalterable. If an apocalypse reads the past typologically, it does not countenance the possibility that its own disclosures are open to typological reinterpretation.[50]

It should be emphasized that these conceptions of prophecy and apocalyptic are modern abstractions and do not designate differences in genre
by which to distinguish an ancient prophetic oracle from an ancient apocalypse. Nevertheless, they are appropriate concepts for use in biblical theology. As I will argue, the canonical process and its precipitate, the Christian Bible, *create* provisional prophecy as a literary effect. And one result of
Paul's incorporation into the canon is that the canon now co-determines
the meaning of Paul's teaching about Israel by reframing Pauline apocalyptic as prophecy. That canonical reframing does not harmonize Paul
with other forms of biblical eschatology, but it does alter the rhetorical cast
of Paul's apocalyptic oracles.

We must bear in mind that the canonical Paul is not simply a scriptural
voice; he is also a character in the Christian Bible. Therefore, instead of fo-
cusing solely on the stories that Paul tells of God, Israel, and the gentiles,
we should attend as well to the canon's own rendering of Paul as God's
spokesman. In this rendering, I suggest, Pauline apocalyptic is recast as
provisional prophetic revelation.

"Story" is to be distinguished here from "narrative," which refers to a
particular telling of a story. Richard Hays has shown how productive this
literary-critical distinction can be when it is applied to Paul's letters,
which, although they are not narratives, do contain bits of narrative and
references to events from which it is possible to construct, for example,
stories of Christ.[51] In a somewhat similar approach, Norman Petersen has
shown how a letter can imply, without narrating, rather complex stories,
and that it is possible to use the Pauline corpus as a whole to construct
Paul's "narrative world" as a symbolic universe structured through story.[52]
In that storied universe, God, Christ, Paul, other believers, and so forth are
all characters, and in the "grammar" of that narrative world, Paul can tell
any number of stories about himself, Israel, Jews and gentiles, the church,
Christians, a master and his slave, and so on.

In using the term *grammar* of Paul's narrative world, I shift to a
metaphor that Hendrikus Boers has applied very fruitfully to Paul's letters.[53] Adapting Noam Chomsky's linguistic theory of generative grammar, Boers seeks to identify the "deep" structures of Paul's thinking that
enable—and, in turn, are expressed by—a variety of "surface" structures
(Paul's verbal discourse). While Boers does not seek to reconstruct *storied*
deep structures, one might posit that when Paul writes, he is always operating with a story at the deep level, to which his surface discursive articu-
lations bear witness. Something like this is what Hays means by the narrative substructure of Paul's argumentation.[54] One might also guess that
Paul operates with a cluster of more or less related, and perhaps even integrated, stories.

In the model advanced by Boers, the deep structure generates various surface expressions, which suggests that a proper analysis may lead us to an identification of the deep structure that is verifiable by its success in accounting for the various surface structures. Likewise, Hays argues that the test of any reconstruction of a narrative substructure is how well it helps us make sense of Paul's arguments. These are exciting proposals, and it is entirely possible that Hays's focused analysis of Gal. 3:1–4:11 or Boers's broader analysis of Galatians and Romans does indeed reveal the presupposed story or the deep convictions belonging to the mind of the historical Paul.

But it is also possible to view the whole matter in a very different way. We may regard a plausible version of the narrative substructure or deep convictional structure as an *apparent* deep structure. Moreover, more than one plausible construction of the apparent deep structure may emerge. A different set of exegetical decisions about Paul's apparent intent may lead to a different construction of the grand story of basic generating principles. When we move to the canonical level, matters may become simplified in some respects but more complex in others. On the canonical plane, we have to do not only with what Paul said (wrote) but also with the field of associations set up by his use of scripture texts, which evoke their own contexts and multiply the semantic possibilities for interpreting his arguments. Moreover, we must consider the semantic effects wittingly and unwittingly produced by the shapers of the canon through the process that eventuates in the final form of the canon. The canonical deep structure of Romans is co-determined by the larger canonical context.

With reference to the *story of Paul* implied by the canon, I focus narrowly on the Paul who makes prophecies about the gentiles and Israel in Romans. In the implied story of the canonical Paul, Paul's expectation of the imminent resolution of history is part of Paul's gospel and informs his conception of his apostolate. Moreover, the promise of that fulfillment is, in the canon, God's own revelation to Paul. That is, in the canonical story of Paul, it is God who tells Paul that the last days have arrived. But the canon also assumes that the world continues beyond the generation of the apostles.

This canonical assumption receives a variety of interpretations by those who shaped the canon over several centuries. But I am not equating the assumption itself with any particular patristic eschatology. It has been observed that the early church of the first several centuries does not seem to have been radically disturbed by what modern scholars term the "delay" or "nonoccurrence" of Christ's heavenly appearance (the Parousia).[55] More precisely, the postapostolic generations of Christians do not seem to have been aware of what modern scholarship rediscovered toward the end of the nineteenth century, namely, the *inaugurated* apocalyptic eschatology of Paul. The idea of the Parousia of Christ was early on divorced from the organic conception of an inaugurated End, and this made it possible for the author of 2 Peter to treat the question of "delay" in terms of the successive ages of history. In fact, it is not even clear that 2 Peter is explaining any so-called delay of a Parousia preached by the apostles as an imminent event in their lifetimes. As 2 Peter frames the problem, the more general view of some is that there will be no end to the created order. In response, 2 Peter delimits the tenure of the created order by insisting that the world will one day arrive at an apocalyptic end.

Second Peter represents only one of a variety of eschatological perspectives in the New Testament. But it is of special interest here because it reflects, within the New Testament itself, a formative moment in the canonical process. It serves to mark the Pauline letters as scripture (2 Peter 3:15–16) and, by implication, to certify itself (and 1 Peter) as scripture (3:1), making it clear that no other letters passing under Peter's name are to be so regarded.[56] The voice of the canonical Peter also signals a general and shared assumption of the Christians who shaped the canon, namely, that history continues in God's providence for generations beyond the time of the apostles. This canonical assumption, in turn, produces interesting literary effects.

In a sense, Ströter perceives one such plausible effect. From the standpoint of his Dispensationalist conception of the canonical story, Ströter assumes that the Bible reckons with many future generations of carnal Israel between the death of Jesus and the end of history. Read on this assumption, Rom. 11:25–29 implies that Jews can be faithful to God only by maintaining their Jewish identity and divine vocation through keeping the Torah through the course of whatever generations intervene before the End.

Ströter does not defend this view by developing a conception of intrascriptural co-determination. He assumes a homogeneity of minds among the historical biblical authors. Hence he never asks how the incorporation of Paul into the Christian canon changes Paul. That question can arise when a canonical approach makes use of genuinely historical-critical investigation in order to show how the canon recontextualizes the revelations of Paul, thus converting them from apocalypses into provisional prophecies.

The New Testament canon, in effect, rewrites Paul's own story of the revelations he received from God. In the canonical story, Paul learns from God that he belongs to that generation of Israel "on whom the ends of the ages have come" (1 Cor. 10:11). But in the canonical story, God's communication is also radically qualified. In the retrospective focus of the Christian Bible, Paul's apocalypse looks like contingent prophecy. Paul appears as one more biblical prophet who discloses a divine word that turns out to be contingent—because disconfirmed. The question is, then, how to understand the abiding truth of the surpassed disclosure.[57]

In an incipiently canonical interpretation of "promise and fulfillment" in the Old Testament, Walther Zimmerli proposes that "the genuine prophet of the Old Testament knows . . . that he is no soothsayer (even though the words of his promise always refer to actual history), because he proclaims the coming work of the one who remains Lord over the way his will is to be realized."[58] The true prophet, according to Zimmerli's characterization, must deliver the word of the Lord "with all certainty," yet "only Yahweh himself can legitimately interpret his promise through his fulfillment, and the interpretation can often be full of surprises for the prophet himself."[59] Whether or not this judgment holds for any of the Israelite prophets in their subjective consciousness, it is a fair description of prophecy as a canonical phenomenon.[60]

For those who eschew harmonizing methods, the concept of the integrity of the Christian canon spells the end of the apocalyptic "must," because every apocalypse is canonically qualified by the prophetic witness to the freedom of God. At the canonical level, apocalyptic undergoes a conversion into prophecy. This happens to Paul. Joined to the Jewish scriptures, Paul's apocalypses acquire the canonical status of prophetic revelation, and Paul the canonical persona becomes a prophet "who proclaims the coming work of the one who remains Lord over the way his will is to be realized." Refigured through recontextualization within the Christian canon, Paul speaks "with all certainty" about Israel, but his revelations now appear to be prophetic signs and not apocalyptic certainties. The one who imitates in his rhetoric God's trick on Israel is himself subject to a divine deception. It turns out that the eschaton did not commence with Christ's death and resurrection; hence the canon itself compels a rethinking of all the metaphors of inaugurated eschatology.

The literary-critical category of recognition (anagnorisis) can help us define more precisely the nature of this canonical effect. In a narrative, recognition scenes are often open to a degree of doubt. What looks like disclosure may be no more than the preparation for a later surprise through another disclosure. Thus, if a moment of recognition entails a surprise, the implied reader has especially good reason to hold open the possibility of some further and more final reversal of the prior disclosure. Even ending recognition scenes can give grounds for doubt.

Terence Cave has carried out a broad-ranging treatment of literary anagnorisis.[61] His central thesis is that "recognition scenes in literary works are by their nature 'problem' moments rather than moments of satisfaction and completion."[62] Cave uses Homer's narrative of the old Greek story of Odysseus as a paradigm case. Odysseus "carries from his fictional origins the threat of imposture."[63] The story of his return, with its recognition plot revolving around his scar, "has to be saturated with signs in order to exorcize the threat, but the saturation sufficiently reveals that it cannot be wholly exorcized."[64] This is not to say that Homer's *Odyssey* does not bring closure to the question of whether it is really Odysseus who returns. "It looks reasonable to maintain," Cave admits, "that most traditional recognition plots afford their readers or spectators ample reassurance: we are meant to believe that the real Odysseus has come home, that horrid transgressions may be brought to light and expiated, that confusion and error can be eliminated."[65] Nevertheless, the very means by which traditional recognition plots bring about such reassurances puts the lie to recognition. Outside of fiction, Cave observes, the fear of anagnoristic deception "can never quite be tranquillized."[66] And in some literature, especially in modern fiction, anagnorisis itself is structured in a way that raises doubts. Thus in literature, as in life, recognition "may easily turn out to be an imposter, claiming to resolve, conjoin and make whole while it busily brings to the surface all the possibilities that threaten wholeness."[67]

The supreme instance of recognition is a divine apocalypse. Paul claims to have been privileged with such a recognition: the revelation of Jesus Christ, in whom Paul recognizes that the end of the Torah and the end of history are already underway. But readers with eyes to see the trick God played on Israel may wonder how Paul can be confident that he himself is not the victim of some undisclosed divine trick. The canon provides its own answer to this question. It certifies Paul as God's true prophet, thus placing boundaries around the question of a divine deception of Paul—a deception, or at least partial opacity, that it nonetheless insinuates between the lines. The Pauline gospel is permeated with "the sense of an ending,"[68] but the reader of the canonical Paul knows that something has gone amiss. The divine revelation to Paul has gone unfulfilled. This impression is not simply the external judgment of a critical reader; it is structured into the Pauline story within the canon itself. The canon rends the apocalyptic fabric of the historical Paul's thought and presents its own, biblical Paul as a prophet whose message of inaugurated cosmic cataclysm and new creation did not materialize as he expected. Thus the canonical Paul preaches with certainty the message of a God who is bound to surprise him. And in the canonical story, a divine surprise is in fact registered—not for Paul the biblical character but for us, his readers.

4

The Right to Be Israel

Speaking to white America in an 1853 address titled "Our Rights as Men," black abolitionist William Watkins produced this play on the identities of Israel and the nations:

> You are the Jews, the chosen people of the Lord, and we are the poor rejected Gentiles. But the times of refreshing are still coming from the presence of the Lord, and we wait, with anxious expectation, the arrival of the auspicious era; for then, we trust, the fullness of the Gentiles will be brought in. . . . Why should *you* be a chosen people more than *we?*[1]

At first sight, it appears that Watkins concedes white America's pretension to be a new Israel. But reading Watkins's speech in its original rhetorical context, we might take his words as ironic. For Watkins's African-American audience, black America was Israel; white America was Egypt.[2] Thus, Watkins's words admit a double reading—one in which Watkins seeks to widen the circle of election, another in which he narrows it by denominating outsiders to the American social contract as true Israel. Or it might be better to read Watkins as implying that America's claim to be a new Israel will remain false until it honors the rights of the true Israel in its midst.

As we have seen, Romans 9—11 admits a similar double reading, depending on how one constructs the logic between the lines of what Paul says. In the first part of this chapter, I sharpen our focus of this double reading by examining the uses of the name Israel in Romans. This sets the stage for a canonical adjudication of the identity of Israel in Romans.

Not All from Israel Are Israel

Perhaps the most enigmatic statement about Israel in Romans appears in Rom. 9:6b, where Paul announces that "not all who are descended from

Israel belong to Israel" (RSV).[3] From this point on, the reader must reckon with the possibility of two different uses of the name Israel in Romans.

For clarity, I designate these two Israels "Israel A" and "Israel B." Given the flow of Paul's argument, it is clear that Israel B is in some sense *true* Israel, but it is not evident what this means. A major question is whether "all Israel" is, by definition, true Israel, thus corresponding exclusively to Israel B, or whether the "mystery" disclosed in 11:25–26 is that not only Israel B but also Israel A will be saved and that the latter is therefore, in some sense, also true Israel.

There are basically two ways in which we can identify Israel A. One is to infer that Paul is talking about Israel A when he refers to the children of Abraham in 9:7, a designation that corresponds to "children of the flesh" in v. 8 and means all of Abraham's literal descendants. In that case, Israel A includes Ishmael and Esau—that is, not simply the Jewish people but all the peoples in the biblical story for whom Abraham is primal patriarch.

A second way to identify Israel A is to conclude that the argument in 9:7–13 is not describing the genealogies of Israel A and Israel B but is simply illustrating God's freedom in election. In that case, the history of election from Abraham to Jacob provides an analogue by which to infer that a similar elective differentiation must also be at work from Jacob onward, that is, within fleshly Israel. That would make Israel A the twelve tribes stemming from Jacob.

The same two approaches produce different possibilities for identifying Israel B. If Israel A is all the literal children of Abraham and vv. 7–13 describe the lines of Israels A and B, then Israel B is some selection from among these literal children. It could be the Jewish nation stemming from Jacob, or it could be a secret elect Israel within but not coterminous with the fleshly descendants of Abraham, Isaac, or Jacob. But if vv. 7–13 do not describe the lines of Israels A and B but provide an analogue for thinking about the election of Israel, then Israel A, as we have seen, is the twelve tribes stemming from Jacob, and Israel B must be some selection from within the line of Jacob.

Moreover, both approaches allow one to infer that by establishing God's radical elective freedom, Paul is paving the way to assert that gentiles, too, may be elected to Israel B. As we have seen, that is one plausible way to construe the drift of Paul's argument in 9:22–29. But it is not clear that the argument either includes or excludes gentiles from Israel B. If the sufficient criterion for inclusion in Israel B were fleshly descent from Abraham, then Ishmael and Esau ought to be part of Israel B. Therefore, since Ishmael and Esau are obviously not part of Israel B, fleshly descent must not be the sufficient criterion for inclusion in Israel B. This raises the question of whether fleshly descent from Abraham, if not a sufficient mark of Israel B, is nonetheless a necessary one. By themselves, the examples of

Ishmael and Esau do not settle this question, and the inference Paul draws is ambiguous: "This means that it is not the children of the flesh who are the children of God, but the children of the promise are counted as descendants" (9:8).

We may also note that in 9:8, "God" replaces Abraham as the father of Abraham's elect descendants. This is significant. While the expression "children of the promise" could mean an elect line within the fleshly seed of Abraham, the development of the argument (9:9–29) emphasizes God's freedom from human constraints and assumptions. The purpose of election depends on this freedom, which, according to vv. 11 and 16, operates apart from human willing and doing. It is but a short step from here to the conclusion that God's freedom in election might also manifest itself in the creation of children of God who stand outside the fleshly line of descent from Abraham. That inductive step is especially short because Paul has already argued much more explicitly (in Romans 4) that Abraham's heirs are not restricted to his fleshly descendants but include those non-descendants who share Abraham's faith.

Diagram 1 represents the various interpretive options we have examined thus far. The numbers designate the five possible uses of the name Israel. The correlations between possibilities for Israel A and possibilities for Israel B are also given with the schematic.

We now extend our analysis of Paul's use of the name Israel by looking at its appearance elsewhere in Romans. It happens that the names Israel and Israelite are confined to chapters 9—11, being found at the following points: 9:4, 6, 27, 31; 10:19, 21; 11:1, 2, 7, 25, 26. In 9:4, Paul calls his kinfolk "Israelites." His description of these Israelites indicates that they fall into Israel as the twelve tribes (A2 or B2 on Diagram 1).

In 9:27, Paul quotes Isaiah's words that "though the number of the children of Israel were like the sand of the sea, only a remnant of them will be saved." A glance at Diagram 1 shows that, in theory, this Israel could be Israel A as the twelve tribes (A2), Israel B as the twelve tribes (B2), or an elect Israel within the twelve tribes (B4). But since Isaiah speaks of an enormous company of Israel, we should rule out B4. If Israel A is the twelve tribes (A2), then the "remnant" is Israel B as an elect group within the twelve tribes (B4). Likewise, if Israel B is the twelve tribes (B2), then the "remnant" is also a selection from within this group (but we would not call it B4, since in this interpretation we already have the identity for B).

Closely parallel with the use of "Israel" in 9:27 are the instances in 11:2 and 11:7 where Paul speaks of Israel in the time of Elijah and again distinguishes a "remnant." The Israel about whom Elijah complains is either A2 or B2. If A2, then the remnant is some form of B; if B2, then the remnant is a selection from within the twelve tribes but is not itself Israel B. Certain features of Paul's argument favor the first option (Israel A as A2 and the

DIAGRAM 1

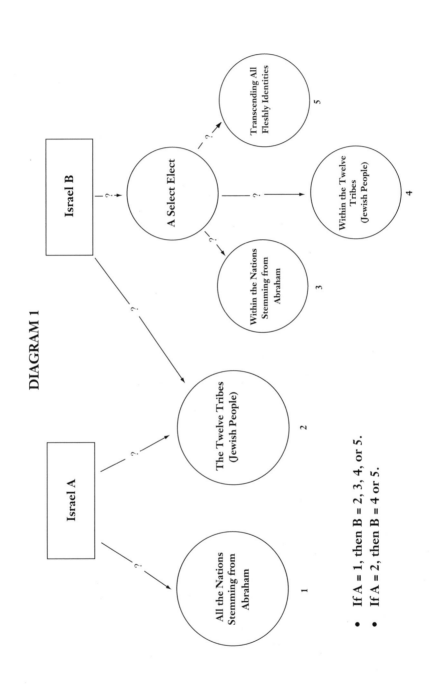

- If A = 1, then B = 2, 3, 4, or 5.
- If A = 2, then B = 4 or 5.

remnant as B2). Paul classes himself as an Israelite according to the A1 class ("descendant of Abraham") and the A2/B2 classes ("of the tribe of Benjamin"). Moreover, he describes the remnant in language that recalls the theme of God's merciful freedom in 9:6–18: "So too at the present time, there is a remnant, chosen by grace" (11:5). Thus, Paul closely associates the "remnant" concept in 11:1–6 with the line (or the logic) of Israel B's election according to 9:6–18.

But to which form of Israel B is Paul referring? With the focus on Elijah's time, "an elect Israel within the twelve tribes" (B4) looks like the best option. But since Paul is making this argument in order to say something about the present (11:5), in which the people of God include both Jews and gentiles, an Israel transcending all fleshly identities (B5) is also a genuine option.

The uses of "Israel" in 9:31, 10:19, and 10:21 refer to the Jewish people under the law and therefore fall under either A2 or B2. A parallel is also present between 9:31 and 11:7, both of which speak of Israel striving for something it failed to obtain. In 9:30–31, Paul says that gentiles have obtained what Israel sought; in 11:7ff., he says that "the elect" have obtained. This suggests that Israel A is 2 and Israel B is 4 or 5, thus reinforcing the impression we got from 11:1–6.

We have examined all the uses of "Israel" and "Israelite" except the two in 11:25–26. We have discovered that the use of the name in 9:1–11:24 encourages the conclusion that Israel A is the twelve tribes (the Jewish people) and Israel B is an elect group within or transcending the Jewish nation. If we adhere consistently to this conclusion, we arrive at the following possibilities for interpreting 11:25–26. First, if "all Israel" (11:26) and Israel B are one and the same, then 11:25 means that a hardening has come in part on a select number of now unbelieving Jews who are destined to be saved. In that case, 11:26 means that this hardening will ultimately be lifted and all Israel (either elect remnant Israel or ecclesial Israel) will be saved. Second, if "all Israel" is not coterminous with Israel B, then true Israel is a sign of hope for a much larger Israel.[4]

Diagram 2 represents the options for identifying Israel A and B in relation to the "all Israel" of 11:26. (Since we have not found the category B3 to be useful, it has been dropped from the schematic.)

In connecting 9:6 with 11:26, one is struck by the parallel in phraseology. "All those from Israel" (9:6) looks like a synonym for "all Israel" (11:26). In that case, although Israel A is not true Israel, yet in some sense it, too, is elect Israel and shares in the identity and destiny of true Israel. But it is also possible to restrict the "all Israel" of 11:26 to some form of Israel B.

A similar possibility for a double reading of divine election is found in the Jewish scriptures themselves. In Gen. 17:18, Abraham asks God to

DIAGRAM 2

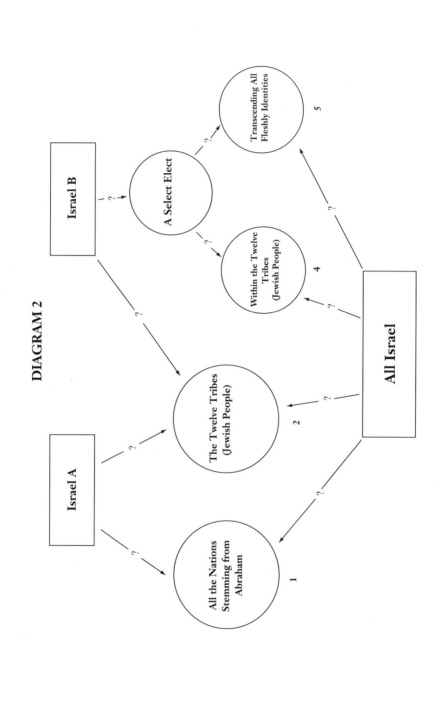

choose Ishmael as his heir, but God demurs, electing to make Ishmael a great nation but not Abraham's heir. By this action, Ishmael becomes a sign of those nations that are *not* the multitude of nations that shall come forth from Abraham in fulfillment of the covenant established through Isaac (Gen. 17:1–22). Nevertheless, the promise of blessing given in Gen. 12:1–3 includes all the families of the earth. Likewise, the reiteration of the promise after the testing of Abraham includes blessing for all the nations of the earth (22:15–18). Further, after God has announced the covenant "in Isaac," Abraham proceeds to circumcise Ishmael, along with all the male slaves of his household, as if to include his whole household—his flesh and blood as well as his slaves—in the covenant from which Ishmael has ostensibly been excluded. It appears, then, that the restriction of heirship to Isaac ends up including Ishmael and envisions blessing for all the nations as its ultimate purpose.

Nevertheless, Genesis also includes statements of the promise that make no mention of blessing for the nations outside the line of promise (13:14–18; 15:1–6, 17–21; 16:10; 17:1–8, 15–20). Thus the canonical form of Genesis is ambiguous in what it says about the status of the nations in relation to the Abrahamic covenant. On one plausible reading, which Paul maximizes, God's primary purpose is to bless all the nations of the earth through Abraham. At the opposite end of interpretation, the blessing for the rest of the nations is a by-product, an excess that displays the abundance of God's benefaction to Abraham. In some versions of this second interpretation, blessing for the other nations depends entirely on how they treat Abraham's seed, for the nations are not co-heirs with Isaac but outsiders and potential enemies (see Gen. 22:17).

Those who know the original context of Gen. 21:12, whose words Paul quotes in Rom. 9:7, may recall the next verse in Genesis, to which I have already alluded: "As for the son of the slave woman, I will make a nation of him also, because he is your offspring" (Gen. 21:13). Since the promise to Abraham includes blessing for the other nations as well, the echo of God's promise to make Ishmael a nation may imply that Ishmael, too, will be blessed through Isaac. We may also recall that the promise to make Ishmael a nation is God's answer to Abraham's prayer "O that Ishmael might live in your sight!" (Gen. 17:18), just as the mystery revealed to Paul about the salvation of all Israel can be taken as God's answer to Paul's prayers:

My heart's desire and prayer to God for them is that they may be saved.

(Rom. 10:1)

For I could wish [or "I could pray"[5]] that I myself were accursed and cut off from Christ for the sake of my own people, my kindred according to the flesh.

(Rom. 9:3)

Paul's kinfolk are carnal Israel, ethnic Israel as conventionally understood by Jews in his day. But Paul has already disturbed conventional definitions of carnal Israel. By the logic of Paul's own definition of Israel A in
9:6–13, carnal Israel ("all from Israel") may include the nations of Ishmael
and Esau (A1), who stand for the nations outside the line of promise. In
that case, carnal Israel includes all the nations. Moreover, if this universal
Israel is to be saved, according to the prophecy of 11:26, then all parties in
the story of election are virtually interchangeable. Although there is only
one true Israel (Israel B), all human beings belong to another Israel, *Abrahamic Israel*. That Israel is also beloved for the sake of the fathers and secure in its own irrevocable gifts and call (cf. Rom. 11:28–29), because God
promised Father Abraham that in him all the nations of the earth would be
blessed (Gen. 12:3; 18:18). The fulfillment of this promise to Abrahamic
Israel is God's ultimate answer to the prayer of Paul for carnal Israel and
also to the prayer of Abraham for the slave woman's son Ishmael—if we so
choose.

A Canonical Adjudication
and Its Rationale

If the Hebrew scriptures present us with a God who chooses Israel for a
special vocation and destiny, Romans requires that we interpreters choose
the identity of Israel from among a circumscribed group of plausible exegetical candidates. We are to make that choice in accord with the purpose
of scripture. I have identified that purpose as fulfillment of the two great
commandments, which the canonical Jesus declares to be the two pillars on
which all of scripture hangs (Matt. 22:37–40). I have also argued that the
second of these commandments (love of neighbor) provides the hermeneutical key to the meaning of the first (love of God) and therefore to the application of both to the interpretation of scripture. To love one's neighbor
as oneself is to share in God's own effort to make and keep life humane.

A starting point for constructing a humane interpretation of Paul's
teaching about Israel in Romans is to reflect on the charge that Paul is
"anti-Jewish" or that his teaching contains potential roots of anti-
Semitism. It is sometimes pointed out that this very question may be inappropriate, since Paul did not see himself as a member of a new religion but
as one Jew talking to other Jews. The historical Paul's critique of Judaism
belongs to an intramural conflict within the diverse matrices that made up
the Judaisms of Paul's day.[6] Admittedly, some Jews who heard Paul's views
about Jesus, the gentiles, and the law may have regarded him as an apostate who was leading people astray. But "anti-Torah," not "anti-Jewish," is
the category in which they were most likely to have framed their conception of Paul.

More important, in locating Paul on the map of ancient Mediterranean religions, historians must locate Pauline Christianity within the pluriformity of various ancient Judaisms, a descriptive task for which "polythetic" taxonomies are more appropriate than "monothetic" ones. In a polythetic taxonomy, "a class is defined as consisting of a set of properties, each individual member of the class to possess a 'large (but unspecified) number' of these properties, with each property to be possessed by a 'large number' of the individuals in the class, but no single property to be possessed by every member of the class."[7] By the logic of a polythetic taxonomy, Paul's definitions of the true Jew and true Israel represent simply one more way by which Jews of Middle Judaism offered competing definitions of what it meant to be a Jew. Hence, whatever other ancient Jews may have thought about Paul's teaching, the historian cannot classify Paul's views as "anti-Jewish."

Nevertheless, people in the Greco-Roman world did not use polythetic modes of classification. Like many people today, they constructed monothetic and hence dichotomizing classes. Therefore, while a history of religions approach may lead us to map Paul *within* the boundaries of ancient Judaism, many Jews (including some Jewish Christians) may have seen Paul as *transgressing* what they identified as the boundary of Jewish identity.

If it could be shown that the historical Paul regarded himself as no longer belonging to Judaism (see, for example, Gal. 1:13), then the label "anti-Jewish" might be applied to his theological polemics (although not to his attitude toward Jewish people in some more general sense). But even then, one would have to show that in defining himself outside Judaism, Paul meant to repudiate Judaism. The evidence on this issue is notoriously difficult to interpret in a unified way, and it may be that Paul himself operated with conflicting self-understandings.

Matters stand differently in the Christian canon, which reframes Paul by making him a witness to a religion distinct from Judaism and which treats his letters as generally valid for the church in all times and places. Moreover, the church lives with a legacy of Christian presumption that Jews and Judaism stand archetypally for all the wrong ways of relating to God, and this legacy continues to influence the reception of Pauline scholarship. Hence any interpretation of Paul's conflicts with his Jewish kinfolk over theological questions is liable to be cast (and even more likely to be received) in terms that make Jews the negative foil of canonical Christian truth. The scholar who argues, for example, that Paul's critique of the law can be best explained if we understand Paul to be attacking "Jewish exclusivism" may appear to be suggesting as well that Judaism warrants Paul's attack. In place of "legalism" and "works righteousness," it is now "religious nationalism" and "Jewish ethnocentrism" that threaten to become the new catchphrases for characterizing ancient Judaism in teaching and preaching from Paul. Admittedly, ancient Jewish attitudes may warrant these characterizations—perhaps more or perhaps less than the attitudes of other groups in the ancient Mediterranean world. But it is not the ancient Scythians or the ancient Greeks who have been immortalized in the canonical Paul for their ethnocentric habits of mind. It is Paul's Jewish kinfolk, whose names now appear to stand in the Christian canon as double signs, signifying at once "Jews," wherever they may be found since the advent of Jesus Christ, and also some evil human tendency, which Christ now besieges as God's agent of redemption. In past theological generations, the "Jewish sin" was taken to be some form of legalism or idolatrous religious self-reliance (works righteousness). Today there is a growing tendency to see it as the inhumanity of ethnocentrism. But whatever the charge, the terms, *Jew, the circumcision, my kindred according to the flesh*, and so forth appear in the Pauline polemics, frozen in the hardened amber of the Christian canon.

It is the indispensable task of historical criticism to restore the diachronic perspective and situate Paul's polemics against the Judaism (and Jewish Christianity) of his day, reconstructing a living context where all sides of the debate can be heard (or at least plausibly imagined). It is the task of canonical criticism to describe the canonical effects of the conversion into scripture of Paul's polemical voice. And it is the function of canonical interpretation to adjudicate the question of the meaning of these terms for the church's constructive use of the canonical Paul.

Given the history of Christian anti-Semitism, compelling moral reasons exist for reinforcing the appropriate historical clarifications and contextualizations of Paul's critique of Jews and Jewish practices, by invoking other available arguments that pit the canonical Paul himself against anti-Jewish Christian habits of mind and rhetoric. I take this to be the moral agenda of the corporate drive in contemporary Pauline scholarship today: to make the case that (1) "all Israel" in Rom. 11:26 is the Jewish people, (2) the salvation of all Israel entails the idea that the Jewish people are irrevocably elect (11:28–29), and (3) the "hardening" of Israel means not that Israel is, on the whole, blind but that God has given Israel a limited blind spot toward Christ. These interpretive judgments, configured together, provide a basis in the canonical Paul for a more respectful and thus a more humane Christian attitude toward Jews and Judaism. In adjudicating the question of Israel in the canonical Romans, I opt to affirm this cluster of exegetical judgments. Among the various plausible interpretive possibilities, they form a synthetic construal that promotes the purpose of scripture, which requires making and keeping the church's life humane toward its Jewish neighbors.

Nevertheless, the question immediately arises whether affirming the irrevocable election of carnal Israel may encourage Christians to adopt less humane attitudes toward other groups, especially those who see themselves in competition with modern Israel or modern Jews. A concern of many Christians today is that to accord the Jewish people a special status over other nations or peoples appears to warrant various kinds of political and cultural favoritism (including a bias in favor of the State of Israel) and threatens to encourage Christian intolerance toward other peoples when the claims of Jews or the interests of the State of Israel are at stake, while fostering attitudes that exempt Jews from the standards that one applies as a matter of course to other groups.[8] To the extent that one presses the idea of an irrevocable election of national Israel in Paul, it appears that one risks undercutting the Pauline theme of divine impartiality. Do we purchase Pauline arguments for a special Christian devotion to Israel at too high a price? Ought Christians not be the moral champions of unqualified divine impartiality toward all, insisting that God does not look with special favoritism on the church, on the Jews, or on a new theopolitical block of "the church with and for Israel"?[9]

Ethnocentrism and other kinds of "we"-centrism come far more naturally to human beings than any form of tolerant and welcoming humanism.[10] Respect for the human dignity of all peoples and of every individual is an attitude requiring nurture and constant defense. Moreover, the Christian contribution to the Western tradition of human rights and egalitarianism has always depended heavily on Paul.[11] Hence any canonical exegesis that undercuts this Pauline base ought to be greeted with caution.

Nevertheless, there is a shadow side to traditional conceptions of Paul's teaching about the unity and equal value of all human beings. The doctrine of humane Christian universalism, with its assumption of divine impartiality toward all human beings, has often been treated as a doctrine about individuals, viewed apart from and even in opposition to their ethnocultural identity. This tendency has thus provided, willy-nilly, a justification for the dismissal of the cultural identity of minority groups by majorities whose cultural identity is secure.[12] For example, by invoking the Pauline slogan "in Christ there is no longer Jew or Greek," ethnoculturally similar Christians who happen to be dominant in a given social environment can use Paul, in effect, to justify themselves when they insist that "others" ought to assimilate to the "common" (dominant) identity for the sake of unity and "the common good." When one's own treasured cultural identity is not threatened, it is easy to quote (and misuse) Paul's universalizing rhetoric against the claims of others. When one feels that one's own cultural identity may be threatened, it is also a temptation to use Paul's words half-rightly—and therefore, wrongly—to criticize the identity politicking of others as inconsistent with the gospel.[13]

In a searching treatment of the question of identity politics from a Jewish perspective, Daniel Boyarin and Jonathan Boyarin suggest that Pauline

Christianity and rabbinic Judaism represent two opposing hermeneutics, each of which has, along with its positive side, a pernicious side that tends to foster intolerance when provided with social power. For this reason it behooves us, the Boyarins urge, to use these two hermeneutics as mutual correctives:

> When Christianity is the hegemonic power in Europe and the United States, the resistance of Jews to being universalized can be a critical force and model for the resistance of all peoples to being Europeanized out of particular bodily existence. When, however, an ethnocentric Judaism becomes a temporal, hegemonic political force, it becomes absolutely, vitally necessary to accept Paul's critical challenge—although not his universalizing, disembodying solution—and to develop an equally passionate concern for all human beings.[14]

The "disembodying solution" is Paul's insistence on the ultimacy of spiritual identity, understood as being in opposition to fleshly identity. To this the Boyarins contrast rabbinic Judaism, which accords spiritual value to the fleshly order, circumcision being the sign of a specific bodily domain where the joys, pleasures, and responsibilities belonging to kinship and its irreplaceable memories are media of the divine presence that valorizes them.

In response, a Christian might observe that very similar notions about embodied life can be found in many forms of Christianity, especially in the modern period. These include, for example, tendencies to sacralize such things as sexuality, the Christian family, and various other "this-worldly" activities and responsibilities. Dietrich Bonhoeffer's "religionless Christianity" (with its attack on "two-sphere" thinking) and Harvey Cox's theology of secularity offer sophisticated examples of this, but they are only two of many indexes of an epochal shift in Western Christianity toward affirmations of embodied life in the world. Nevertheless, the Boyarins have caught the dominant accent in Paul. According to the Pauline model, Christ relativizes kinship identities in favor of spiritual "households of God," to which Christians owe their primary familial allegiance. The question is whether this understanding of the "new creation" in Christ stands inherently opposed to any claim that the God who loves all human beings without partiality loves them also in their ethnocultural particularities.[15]

In answering this question, we may begin by recalling the thesis that Paul does not resolve the tension between the particularism of fleshly Israel's election and the impartial universalism of the new people of God. According to this view, God does not renege on the divine pledges made to the Jewish people as Israel, but God is also not bound by those pledges to abstain from constituting a new people in which there is "no distinction between Jew and Greek." From this one might draw the inference (even if Paul himself does not) that God loves the Jewish people in their fleshly particularity and not simply as a piece of abstract humanity. But if that inference follows, then the logic of divine impartiality implies that God must love the sociocarnal particularity of other peoples too.

Paul expresses his own kinship passions for carnal Israel in Rom. 9:1–3:

> I am speaking the truth in Christ—I am not lying; my conscience confirms it by the Holy Spirit—I have great anguish in my heart. For I could wish that I myself were accursed and cut off from Christ for the sake of my people, my kindred according to the flesh.

The implication of such a statement is a strong valorization of the passions that bind people together in ethnic identity, seeing that the rhetorical force of what Paul says depends on the tacit assumption that special love for one's own people is a common human passion.[16]

C. H. Dodd interpreted Paul's prophecy of carnal Israel's salvation (11:26) in just this sense but dismissed it as contrary to the larger argumentative logic of Romans. According to Dodd, that logic asserts a sweeping universalism and therefore stands in tension with Paul's patriotism, since "the arguments by which Paul asserts the final salvation of Israel are equally valid (in fact are valid only) if they are applied to mankind at large."[17] Hence we would do better to reinterpret the thought of 11:26 as an affirmation of the "high destiny" promised to humanity in "all the great religions."[18]

I construe the pieces of Paul's logic a bit differently. Rather than dismissing Paul's love for carnal Israel as unworthy of his gospel, we may reframe it. Paul's passion for his kinfolk, like other human passions, must be rightly ordered by a constantly renewed and discerning mind (Rom. 12:1–2)—one mark of that mind being an enlarged vision of God's own passionate love for all human beings. Regarded in this light, Romans 9—11 is, at least in part, Paul's effort to rightly order his own passions for his Jewish kinfolk together with the love he so often expresses in his letters for the saints in Christ. The latter are his spiritual kin. Moreover, those spiritual kin represent the world, the "all" of humanity to whom Paul is dedicated by the love and mercy of God. In this connection we may note 2 Cor. 5:13–15, where Paul confesses that what may look like "madness" in his conduct (v. 13) is, in fact, an expression of divine love, inspiring in Paul a passionate love not only for the Corinthians but also for the world: "For the love of Christ urges us on, because we are convinced that one has died for all."

But it is not only his love for the world that Paul describes as divinely inspired. Paul also exhibits his love for carnal Israel as a divinely inspired passion. The references in 9:1 to speaking "in Christ" and to the witness of the Spirit imply divine approval of that passion. Furthermore, by adjudicating the identity of "all Israel" in 11:26 to mean "the Jewish people as a whole," we make the promise of the salvation of the Jewish people a divine answer to Paul's ardent prayer for his own people (10:1). In the end, Paul implies, "God will honor my passionate love for my own people." This further suggests that God, too, has a passional love for Israel.

The idea that God is ardent for the Jewish people is confirmed by resonances from scripture quotations in Romans 9—11. What I accept as an echo of scripture from Hosea in Rom. 9:25–26 recalls God's passion for his divorced wife, carnal Israel. And in 10:21, the "outstretched arms" of God express a similar divine passion for Israel. Then there is Paul's description in 11:2 of carnal Israel as the people whom God "foreknew," an expression that bespeaks an ancient intimacy between God and Israel.[19] Added to this is Paul's assertion that Israel is "beloved" for the sake of the forefathers, presumably Abraham, Isaac, and Jacob—Jacob (Israel) being the one whom God "loved" over Esau (Rom. 9:13, quoting Mal. 1:2–3).

It is a mistake, therefore, to treat the tension in Romans between divine impartiality and the irrevocable election of Israel solely as a conflict between divine faithfulness to promises made to Israel and God's impartial love for all human beings. A conflict also arises between two divine loves. It is easy to overlook this if one takes the language of righteousness, faithfulness, and impartial love literally but treats the passional language used of God's relation to Israel as if it were mere anthropomorphism. In fact, there has been a tendency in Pauline interpretation to treat this language of divine passion as if it were figurative, perhaps to avoid an interpretive conflict with Paul's assertions about God's universal and impartial love. Thus, if Paul affirms that God remains faithful to the promises made to the patriarchs, it is assumed that Paul means this literally and that he is ascribing the virtue of faithfulness to God. But when Paul says that God uses the gentiles to provoke Israel to jealousy, Pauline scholars have tended to resist the implication that Paul casts God as jealous for Israel's love, as if God had a special passion for Israel as Israel. Likewise, when Paul says that the gospel makes Israel "enemies," while election makes them "beloved," the passional side of these assertions is ignored or absorbed into abstract universalities. The terms *beloved* and *enemies* are treated as signs of the conflict between God's pledges to the patriarchs and God's universal mercy, which knows no special love for any particular people. That is, Paul's God is permitted to be passionate only in the sphere of universal love. Hence, God's election of Israel is seen as a dispassionate act that serves the purposes of universal divine love.

But if we are prepared to describe Paul's God as torn between the claims of irrevocable pledges made to Israel and the claims of impartiality toward all human beings, then we ought to recognize the evidence that Paul's God is also torn between two loves. If we assume that "all Israel" (in 11:26) is ethnic Israel, then God's passion for Israel is the best explanation of why the election of Israel requires the salvation of the nation as a whole. Paul has already established that God is fully justified and unimpeachable in his faithfulness when he inflicts wrath on carnal Israel (Rom. 3:1–8). Thus, God's *justice* does not require that God save all of carnal Israel. Hence the conviction that accounts for Paul's faith that all Israel has a share in the age to come must be the like rabbinic belief that God has a special and undying passion for carnal Israel.

The concern to guard against inferences that undermine divine impartiality is well placed. But I have a special reason for pressing the evidence that Paul assumes God's special love for Israel. The possibility of any Christian claim, based on Paul, that God loves human beings not simply in their common humanity but also in their corporate particularities (or "difference," as one likes to say today) hinges on the nature of God's love for carnal Israel. The reason lies in the logic that the only way to resolve the tension between divine impartiality toward all human beings and the special election of Israel is to infer that, with God, *every people has the right to be Israel.*

We must be clear that this resolution establishes a new tension on another level. Unlike Dodd, I am not contending for a logical resolution that absorbs Israel's ethnic particularity without remainder into the abstract notion of an elect humanity. On the contrary, I am proposing that God's special and irrevocable love for carnal Israel helps us interpret the impartiality of divine universalism. God is impartial in loving human beings not only in their similarities to one another but also in their differences, including the ethnocultural differences that separate human beings into distinct peoples.

This is by no means to suggest that everything that makes the peoples of the world different from one another wins divine approbation. Rather, it is to recognize that the good in all and in each is liable to be divided. Not all good differences can be honored by the divine love that treasures not only similarities but also what is unrepeatably unique. This produces the conditions for potential conflict between God's general love for humanity as a whole and God's special loves for distinct peoples in their sometimes incommensurable differences. Christian affirmation of this double love of God requires a constructive Christian ethic that does justice to both its sides. Insofar as we are imitators of God, we will be rightly torn by more than one good love, as Paul was.

It is important to reemphasize that the preceding interpretation is a constructive adjudication, informed by moral judgments lying largely outside the conceptual frameworks of Paul. I am not claiming that Paul was dealing with modern concerns, much less that he was guided by the same insights into human identity that inform modern discussions of this complex subject. Rather, I have used my own ethical sense, informed by modern discussions, to justify a specific interpretation—or integrated complex of interpretive decisions—as most conducive to a humane use of Romans by the church in the late twentieth century. My canonical adjudication is, of course, open to critique—not only by other Christians but also by non-Christians, including Jews. But it should also be obvious that the ethical sensibilities guiding my adjudication have been informed not only by Christian thinkers and Christian experience but also by the thinking and experiential witness of non-Christians, including Jews.

I make this point for two reasons. First, I am loath to leave the impression that my Christian Paul trumps the Boyarins' rabbis—as if I meant to argue that Paul turns out to be more comprehensive than they because he encompasses the virtues of both universalism and particularism. The Boyarins' unfolding of the rabbinic perspective inspired my interpretation of Paul, supplying a conceptual framework that allowed me to see Paul's text in a way that let the theme of divine passion in Paul come to light and exert a constitutive influence in my adjudication of universalism and particularism in Romans. By the same token, a modern rabbi can learn from Paul to see the Torah differently, as Jacob Neusner has done.[20] Second, I wish to reiterate that arguing from scripture does not shut out the opinions and experiences of the world, as if the result of canonical interpretation were a product to be correlated with concrete life in the world only after an interpretation has left the exegetical assembly line. Not only is it probably impossible to construct very many (if any) significant theological arguments from scripture without drawing "data, warrants, and backing"[21] from outside scripture, but it also runs against the humane purpose of scripture to try to escape these outside influences; for, while scripture is to inform and correct one's understanding of what it means to love God and one's neighbor as oneself, we saw in chapter 3 that knowledge of what this double love means also provides a methodologically prior sense of the purpose of scripture in its hermeneutical function—a sense that ought to play a decisive role in how we adjudicate the meaning of scripture for the church.

Literal Israel as
Symbol and Metaphor

I closed the first section of this chapter by pressing Paul's logic in the direction of a universal concept of Israel. I proposed to call this universal Israel "Abrahamic Israel," in distinction from the Jewish people as true Israel. I further suggested that we could equate the "all who are descended from Israel" in Rom. 9:6b with the "all Israel" of 11:26. But in the second section, I opted to interpret "all Israel" in 11:26 as the Jewish people. I still contend that all parties in Paul's story are elect, but my hermeneutical adjudication requires that if we apply the name Israel to others, we can do so only metaphorically. Hence we must assume that the Jewish people are literal Israel, as the "vehicle" that redescribes the "tenor" of any such metaphorical application.[22] This means that the sign "Israel" is not to be treated as a cipher, as if the literal, conventional sense of this sign were mere "surface," betokening a deeper, nonliteral substance.

But in what sense are Jews literal, carnal Israel? Daniel Boyarin argues that in rabbinic semiosis, "carnal" carries a symbolic but not an otherworldly sense.[23] Literal flesh stands by metonymy for this-worldly orders of being in God's creation. Circumcision is a mark of "natural or naturalized membership in a particular people" and, as such, is "the center of salvation."[24] Moreover, natural and naturalized membership in Israel are both *literal* ways of being a descendant of Abraham. Circumcision as a sign of natural, fleshly descent stands for genealogy. The cut in the penis represents the bond of kinship through blood, "blood" being a synecdoche for the flesh that makes Jews literal children of Abraham. But, clearly, *literal* here is an ambiguous term. While it means literal genealogical descent, such descent is in all sorts of ways fictional. Few Jews can claim literal genealogy through Abraham. Hence, factually speaking, literal descent from Abraham is a fiction symbolized by circumcision. Nevertheless, this fiction does not vitiate the meaning of circumcision as a fleshly sign of fleshly kinship in God's people. The fleshly sign "circumcision" means literal kinship, with all its carnal aspects (including descent), but it does not mean literal biological descent, since circumcision also effects "naturalized" membership in a particular people. Here "naturalized" carries full force. Conversion to Judaism makes one a natural Jew, part of the *flesh* of Israel, in the real sense of the term as a descriptor of the carnal family of Israel.[25]

The significance of circumcision as a fleshly thing is thus a literal nonliteral significance.[26] Circumcision in the rabbinic semiology confers value on extended family kinship—including tribal and ethnic determinations of fleshly kinship—and also on the flesh in general. But flesh as kinship is constructed socially and therefore does not refer to the merely biological. I understand this to be Daniel Boyarin's significant point when he says that, within the symbolic universe of the rabbis, circumcision confers value on social flesh; it does not point to some other, "more valuable" world, opposed to the sociocarnal order. Moreover, for the rabbis, the social flesh sanctified by circumcision is the flesh of Israel—that particular people which enjoys a fleshly and even an "erotic" life with God.[27] Or, as Jacob Neusner observes, when modern Jews identify themselves as Israel, they claim to be like Israel of old and thus they invoke a social *metaphor*.[28] What Neusner means is that Jews cannot validate their identity as Israel from facts that exist apart from their own claim to the heritage of Israel.[29] In the end, the criteria that determine who counts as an Israelite are theological; they form a theology of social identity that is metaphorically constructed.

In summary, literal Israel as the vehicle in a metaphorical redescription of the church, or of any other people, is not "mere" letter but a symbolically charged literal sense. Hence the metaphorical use of the name Israel by Christians is only as rich or hermeneutically powerful as their grasp of the literal symbolism that belongs to this name as used by true Israel, the people of the Torah.

Nationalism and National
Differentiation in Pauline Perspective

Throughout this study, I have been using the term *gentiles* to translate ἔθνη. I have avoided using the proper noun *Gentiles*, which would suggest that non-Jewish people go by a single, proper name in Paul. But the translation "gentiles" is also misleading, since *gentiles* carries the predominant meaning "non-Jews." The term ἔθνη, however, means "peoples" or "nations." It is true that Hellenistic Jews often used the term ἔθνη to differentiate Israel from other peoples, with the result that ἔθνη often corresponds to the Hebrew *goyim*. But Greek-speaking Jews could also describe Israel as an ἔθνος, one of the ἔθνη. Thus the ἔθνη can be either "the nations" in general or the nations of the world to which Israel does not belong. Therefore we ought to render ἔθνη consistently "nations" (or "peoples") in Romans and allow context to determine the specific sense or particular nuance.[30]

The translation "gentiles" is also misleading in another way. "Gentiles" suggests an undifferentiated mass of people and thus occludes the plurality designated by ἔθνη: nation*s*, people*s*. At points, Paul distinguishes Jews from other peoples by lumping the latter under a single *name:* Greek. In such instances, "Greek" stands for non-Jew in a differential pairing (Rom. 1:16; 2:10; Gal. 3:28; Col. 3:11). "Greek" is a proper name for a particular people, and in Paul's day it stood also for a desirable and widely adopted cultural identity, one that many Jews bore with much pride. Paul's use of the pairing "Jew and Greek" may therefore serve as an oblique reminder to us not only that non-Jewish peoples are not simply "gentiles" (but have names of their own) but also that the cultural identities signified by these names undergo continual intermixing in a social environment in which some hybrid identities carry more prestige than others.

In a famous study, Martin Buber contends that while Paul speaks of Jews and Greeks, he never does so "in connexion with the reality of their nationalities."[31] Paul is "only concerned with the newly-established community, which by nature is not a nation."[32] There is much truth in this judgment, but it requires some qualification. In Romans, the nations are not an undifferentiated mass of non-Jewish individuals (gentiles); nor are they a single non-Jewish people (the Gentiles). While Paul can naturally describe them collectively, his missionary strategy treats them as different peoples, ranged according to geographical homelands. The implied assumption of his missionary itinerary is that the full number of the nations cannot "come in" through apostolic agency in a single "gentile" locale, even a cosmopolitan one. The mission to the nations has a geo-international scope, one for which biblical maps exist.

Many scholars have seen a connection in Paul between his conception of his mission to the nations and scripture prophecies about the nations making a pilgrimage to Zion in the last days.[33] It has also been plausibly argued that the collection for the saints at Jerusalem symbolizes, in Paul's mind, the fulfillment of these prophecies—a fulfillment that is to prepare for the salvation of all Israel and the culmination of history. Roger Aus has gone even further, arguing that Paul derived from scripture not only the general idea but also the specific identities and geographical localities of the various nations to be included. Aus thinks that Paul was guided by texts such as Isaiah 60, Isaiah 66, and Psalm 68. According to Aus, these passages of scripture led Paul to plan a mission to Spain, the "end of the earth," as prelude to the end of history.[34]

Whether or not Aus is right in his rather precise reconstruction of Paul's interpretation of scripture, he is correct to emphasize the ways in which Romans implies a geographical dimension of the "full number of the gentiles." In announcing his plan to visit the Roman Christians and be "sent on" by them for missionary work in Spain, Paul asserts that he has "no more room" in the regions he has already evangelized (15:23–24). This recalls his claim that "from Jerusalem as far around as Illyricum I have fully proclaimed the good news of Christ" (15:19). In the same context, Paul also mentions his policy of preaching in unevangelized territories, "so that I do not build on someone else's foundation" (15:20). While this explains why Paul has not yet visited the Roman church and why he assures his audience that he has no designs on the apostolic territory of others, it fails to explain why he plans to evangelize Spain—logistically a rather daunting undertaking, as Robert Jewett has shown.[35] Paul's claim that he has thoroughly evangelized the regions marked out by Jerusalem to the east, Illyricum to the north, makes sense only if Paul is founding Christian communities that will make up the full number of the nations not only numerically but also geographically. And in that case, the full number of the gentiles means the divinely appointed number of *nations* as distributed throughout the inhabited world. It is difficult to define precisely Paul's image of that world, but it is probably a composite of the Roman Empire and the map of the world a Hellenistic Jew might have constructed from the scriptures.

The geographical scope of Paul's mission suggests that we ought to translate ἐν πᾶσιν τοῖς ἔθνεσιν in Rom. 1:5 as "among all the nations" and τὸ πλήρωμα των ἐθνῶν in 11:25 as "the full number of the nations." The complete number of gentiles cannot be gathered from only one locale, because ἔθνη symbolizes not undifferentiated gentiles but various, distinct peoples coming from their respective homelands. Of course, Asia Minor itself was ethnically heterogeneous and included populations from many different parts of the world. Nevertheless, geographical differentiation in Paul's missionary plans symbolizes differentiation among the nations and thus establishes the value of ethnic difference within the scope of the Pauline mission. Paul seeks out representatives from various lands and peoples to stand for the inclusion of the gentiles in God's saving work toward all.

The scriptural texts adduced by Aus identify various nations located on a Jewish mental map of the world. If Paul envisions the ultimate inclusion of all humanity in election, these nations represent humanity in its national differentiation. Nothing Paul says indicates that he is operating according to some fixed list of peoples to be evangelized, according to the scriptures. But the journey to Spain is well accounted for by the idea that scripture prophesies that various far-off lands will share in God's blessing and pay homage to the God of Israel. One of those far-off lands is Tarshish, which was identified as Spain in Paul's day. Tarshish/Spain is the end of the earth in one direction; the global scope of Paul's westward mission beckons him there.

If it is important to God that the representatives of the variety of nations be included in the fullness of the gentiles, then it follows that God in some sense honors national differentiation in the gospel. Just as "neither Jew nor Greek" presupposes both Jew and Greek, so "neither Scythian nor Ethiopian"[36] would presuppose both Scythian and Ethiopian. Therefore, while the ultimate eschatological goal may be unity without differentiation, the missionary way to that goal includes strategies that recognize and, to a certain extent, affirm a divine recognition of ethnic differentiation. Here is a further warrant, now from a different angle, for concluding that the God who loves all human beings without partiality loves them also in their ethnocultural particularities.

The multinational churches of the Pauline mission are signs of God's election of all the nations. I have argued that if God treats all alike, then in Paul's story of God's dealings with Jews and gentiles, what holds for Israel ought to hold equally for the nations. God ought to cherish the ethnic particularity of each people just as God cherishes Jewish flesh; God ought to be extending vocations to other nations; and God's call to non-Jewish nations ought to be irrevocable in the same way as God's gifts and call to Israel are unsurpassable. I do not imagine that the historical Paul, who lived intellectually on the brink of an imminently expected end of the world, ever entertained the idea that the identity and vocation of Israel were typologically transferable to other nations. But canonical Paul must be ordered in relation to scripture as a whole, which provides further warrants for this typology.

In Amos 9:7, God asks Israel, "Are you not like the Ethiopians to me, O people of Israel? . . . Did I not bring Israel up from the land of Egypt, and the Philistines from Caphtor and the Arameans from Kir?" This is not the only place in the Prophets where a divine election of other nations is proposed. As Michael Fishbane points out, in the Hebrew (MT) version of Isa. 19:19–25, we meet a typological application to another nation of Israel's self-identity. Fishbane calls it an "audacious inversion and transfer of a national tradition of redemption to the very people—the Egyptians—who were its original enslaver."[37] After his analysis of the text, Fishbane concludes that here "the phenomenon of biblical historical typologies is brought to its conceivable limit":

> For hereby the subject-matter has been inverted to such an extent that just that redemptive event which constituted Israel's particular destiny has become the prototype by which a more universal, messianic reconciliation is envisaged. Egypt, the first oppressor, will one day have its share in an exodus-type event; indeed, teaches the prophet, the new exodus will be nothing less than the redemption of the original enemy in a manner typologically similar to the foundational redemption of YHWH's chosen people. In fact the typological daring on this point is so complete that even the older notion of Israelite chosenness is qualified: for in v. 25 Isaiah projects a time when Egypt, like Israel, will also be called "my people" (עמי) by Yahweh (cf. Exod. 3:10).[38]

The presence of both Romans and Isaiah in the Christian Bible produces an intra-canonical effect of each upon the other. The texts mutually reinforce one another, providing us with a canonical basis for the teaching that the God of Israel elects not only Israel but other nations as well. Paul's interpretation of the scriptural axiom of divine impartiality supplies a strong theological warrant for construing Isaiah's bold typology in a universal sense. But there are also effects in the other direction—effects of Isaiah on Romans.

One of these effects is the way in which Isaiah reinforces the exegetical possibility that Rom. 9:22ff. does not class Pharaoh and the Egyptians as vessels of wrath. In chapter 2, I showed that we have an instance of rhetorical co-deliberation in 9:22ff. From that co-deliberation a moment of suspense arises about whether God has created vessels of wrath. The introduction and development of this possibility suggest that Paul is indeed claiming that God has created some people to be instruments destined for destruction, their sole purpose being to serve the interests of certain other vessels of mercy. Nevertheless, I have opted to adjudicate the question of the identity of "all Israel" in 11:26 in a way that requires the complementary exegetical decision that Romans 11 supplies a surprise sequel to 9:22ff. The effect of this sequel is to overturn the impression that the majority of Israelites are lumped together with Pharaoh as vessels of wrath. Moreover, if God has not prepared unbelieving Israelites as vessels of wrath, the logic of divine impartiality requires the conclusion that God has not prepared any gentiles as vessels of wrath. All are elected to mercy (11:32). That would include even Pharaoh, Israel's archetypal enemy.

We can now hear an echo of Isa. 19:19–25 on the canonical level of Romans 9.[39] Here are the closing words of the prophet's oracle:

> On that day Israel will be the third with Egypt and Assyria, a blessing in the midst of the earth, whom the LORD of hosts has blessed, saying, "Blessed be Egypt my people, and Assyria the work of my hands, and Israel my heritage."
>
> (Isa. 19:24–25)

In the co-determining witnesses of Romans and Isaiah, the canonical record of God's activity with and for Israel implies a larger canonical story. If narrated, that story would tell how God has been and will be with and for other nations, in ways similar to God's being with and for Israel.

Of course, Assyria is no more, and one would be hard pressed to reconstruct an ethnocultural genealogy that shows modern Egypt to be the same nation or people as the Egypt of Isaiah's day. As we have seen, even the claim of modern Jews to be Israel is a social metaphor; that metaphor holds true because Jews have reclaimed again and again, beyond the epochal breaks and ruptures of history, the heritage of biblical Israel, embodied above all in the oral and written Torah. Therefore the literal sense of Isaiah's prophecy about Assyria, Egypt, and Israel was rendered unfulfillable long ago, joining the ranks of the many deferred and disconfirmed promises of God that dot the landscape of Jewish and Christian scripture.

A "Political" Interpretation of Romans 11:19: "Making Room" for the Gentiles

God has been and will be with and for other nations in ways similar to God's being with and for Israel. In Rom. 11:11–36, Paul describes a divine dialectic by which God deals justly and mercifully with Jews and other nations. Paul conceives himself as an agent of this process. Thus, in 11:13–14, Paul explains to his readers, as Stanley Stowers aptly paraphrases, "Yes, I am addressing you gentiles in this letter *but* you should understand that my very ministry to the gentiles has direct relevance to the salvation of my fellow Jews and their salvation to your own."[40] Paul is playing politics here, and he suggests that his missionary strategy has something to do with God's own work of "breaking off branches," as the simile in 11:17–24 has it. It also has something to do with God's "hardening" of Israel. God has a political strategy for dealing with Jews and gentiles, one whose purpose is that gentiles and, ultimately, all Israel might receive mercy (11:25–32).

A clue to God's politics is found in 11:19, a statement from Paul's extended simile of the olive tree. By hardening and in this way "breaking off" the contemporary branches of the olive tree, God makes room for the other nations. It is Paul's imaginary gentile interlocutor who draws this inference from Paul's argument: "Branches were broken off in order that *I* might be grafted in." Paul agrees (καλῶς), but he rejects his interlocutor's implication that this correct insight supplies grounds for gentile boasting over Jews. To counter this implication, Paul offers a further explanation of why the Jewish branches were broken off (because of their unbelief), but he leaves uncommented that aspect of his interlocutor's explanation with which he expresses agreement. That is, Paul objects to the presumptuously emphatic "I" (ἐγώ)[41] but assents to the logic, "in order that" (ἵνα), of the interlocutor's assertion.

The interlocutor states a half-truth, and it is our task to understand the meaning of the truthful half. Branches were broken off *in order that* the nations might be grafted in. This implies, first of all, that the pruning of some Jewish branches removes an impediment to the inclusion of the nations. From this implication we might draw one of the following interpretive conclusions:

1. The number of the elect is fixed, filled up by Israelites, so that any inclusion of the nations requires an excision of elect Jews.
2. In view of Jewish unfaithfulness, God has decided to give the inheritance to the nations and therefore prunes the Jewish branches from the tree of the patriarchs to effect this supersession.
3. In order that Jews will not dominate gentile Christians and require them to Judaize, God has temporarily pruned the vast majority of Israelites to make what we might call "political space" for those of other nations.

Of these three, the third interpretation is the only one that makes sense if "all Israel" in 11:26 is taken as referring to (or at least including) Paul's kinfolk as a whole. Given that assumption, the first interpretation is ruled out for the following reason: if Paul's kinfolk as a whole are to be saved, then there *is* room in *election* for all the branches of carnal Israel, together with the fullness of the gentiles. That is, no fixed number of "elect Israel" is present within carnal Israel. The second interpretation is excluded for a different reason: if the Jewish branches are to be grafted back on again, then the purpose of their excision is not to exclude them but to include the gentiles. God's purpose ("that [the gentiles] might be grafted in") must therefore be to make room for the gentiles through a temporary exclusion of

Jews. This suggests the logic of the third option. The mass of Israel is to
be shut outside while the gentiles "come in." Then the multitudes of Israel
will come *back* in.

To situate the story of God's politics in a larger canonical context, we
may turn to Galatians 2. An intracanonical interpretation requires that we
read Paul's history-like narratives in Galatians the way we read realistic fiction, accepting the text's own version of the "history" rather than interro-
gating the text to establish facts behind the text's rendition of that history.[42] As part of the Christian canon, Galatians 2 now supplies part of the
canonical story of the gentile mission. In a constructive canonical interpretation, it is therefore appropriate to interpret Rom. 11:19 within the
context of this canonical story. The text makes excellent sense when we
do so.

Paul reports that when he and Barnabas brought Titus to Jerusalem, the
Jerusalem church authorities (Gal. 2:6) did not "compel" Titus to be circumcised, even though Titus had a gentile father (Gal. 2:1–3). This story
is revealing because it suggests that the Jerusalem church possessed the authority to require circumcision of Titus. Paul may not have recognized the
legitimacy of this Jerusalem authority, but he assumes that the "acknowledged pillars" (2:9; cf. 2:2, 6) possessed such authority when he observes
that "even Titus, who was with me, was not compelled to be circumcised"
(2:3). Paul's use of the word *compel* suggests that the authority of Jerusalem
in matters of the law is so powerful that Paul is not in a position to coun-
termand a Jerusalem decision to have Titus circumcised. Paul can publicly
refuse to acknowledge Jerusalem authority, but his protest is not likely to
carry weight with the rest of the church.

We find very similar conditions in the story of Paul's visit to the church
at Antioch (Gal. 2:11–14). There the presence of a party from James threatens the law-free ethos in which Jews and gentiles are communing together
in Christ. Under the eyes of the James party, the Jewish Christians at Antioch abandon table fellowship with the gentiles. Paul interprets their action
as "compelling" the gentiles to "Judaize" (2:14). It is true that the use of the
strong verb *compel* may exaggerate, reflecting less the actual behavior of the
Jews at Antioch than what the opponents at Galatia are demanding of the
gentiles there.[43] Nevertheless, to carry rhetorical force, the story about Antioch must strike Paul's readers as plausible. At least they must be able to
imagine that the separatist practice of the Jews at Antioch put strong pressure on the gentiles there to Judaize—pressure that amounted to compul-
sion. Thus the narrative of the Antioch incident implies that the Jerusalem
leaders exercised authority over followers of Jesus beyond the immediate
locale of Jerusalem. Whatever the historical reality, the implication of Jerusalem authority belongs to the narrative assumptions that make the story
work (lend it verisimilitude). It is this implied narrative assumption that

forms part of the relevant canonical context by which I hope to illumine Rom. 11:19.

I imagine that Paul has reflected as follows: if the relatively small number of Jewish converts to Christ (the Jerusalem church) can create big troubles for the Pauline mission to the gentiles, what would a massive conversion of the nation of Israel have done to that mission! In that consideration lies the clue to what Paul goes on to explain as a divine hardening of Israel. God, Paul implies, has pruned the mass of living Israelites from the "tree" where the promises made to the patriarchs are now being fulfilled, so that these Israelites do not join the church and then dominate the gentiles, compelling Judaizing assimilation, excluding gentiles from assuming positions of status and authority, and effectively curtailing any significant incorporation of gentiles into the new people of God in Christ.

In saying I *imagine* that Paul interpreted the signs of his time in this way, I mean no more than that this interpretation provides a plausible explanation of an otherwise puzzling implication about limited "room" in the tree of election. Thus, as I have divined it, God makes political space for the gentiles by separating the mass of Israel from "us whom he has called, not from the Jews only but also from the Gentiles" (9:24). This separation is temporary and strategic: "until the full number of the gentiles has come in" and "thus all Israel will be saved" (11:25–26). In this political interpretation, the "thus" (οὕτως) of 11:26 acquires a meaning that we have not yet considered: it suggests that salvation for Israel happens when Israel is brought into egalitarian community with those it counts as outsiders and inferiors. Without simply equating such communion of Jews and gentiles with salvation, we may conclude that part of the transformative divine work of salvation involves each party discovering and affirming the divine election of the other.[44]

Paul's story of the olive tree assumes the privileged position of his kinfolk in a particular frame of reference, which I here examine in its social aspect. With respect to would-be gentile converts to the faith of Abraham, Isaac, and Jacob, Paul's kinfolk are potential power brokers. The social weakness and vulnerability of various Jewish groups in the Roman world lies outside the scope of the olive-tree story, which focuses more narrowly on the incorporation of a tiny gentile church into that tree which stands, so to speak, in the midst of a much larger and more robust Israel. As an agent in this story, Paul establishes gentile Christian communities outside the interest of the synagogue, but he is able to do so only because the synagogue does not claim these gentiles for itself.[45] The hardening of the nation as a whole makes political space for these gentiles, whose independent spiritual flourishing, apart from the approbation and supervision of Israel, is also a sign of the full equality of gentiles with Jews as elect children of God.

Conclusion

Divine impartiality refracted through the sign of Israel means that God cherishes the varied flesh of human beings in their concrete social identities, formed by unrepeatable histories and unique memories. Among God's many children, each people turns out to be like Israel, God's favorite child. The church, attentive to the canonical witness of Paul and Isaiah, is not to expropriate to itself the right to be "Israel" but is to bestow that right freely on the peoples of the world, while honoring the people of the Torah as original and true Israel. In this way the church may use scripture to make and keep itself humane according to the purpose of scripture.

It is now fitting to consider how the Matthean definition of the aim of scripture is enlarged for us by Luke 10:25–37, where Jesus presents the example of a despised outsider in order to explain to a Jewish lawyer who one's "neighbor" is. Samaritans are the lawyer's neighbor. They, too, we may now add, are loved like Israel, treasured as the apple of God's eye. Moreover, the Samaritans—or, at least, some Samaritans—may prove to be like Israel in another sense, since being Israel is also a vocation, just as being neighbor is the exemplary vocation of the Samaritan in Jesus' parable. The Samaritan is neither Jew nor Christian; rather, he is the *outsider neighbor* who teaches both Jews and Christians what it means to fulfill the second of the two great commandments and, in that fulfillment, to assume the outsider's vocation as Israel. In the words of Emmanual Levinas:

> For equality to make its entry into the world, beings must be able to demand more of themselves than of the other, feel responsibilities on which the fate of humanity hangs, and in this sense pose themselves problems outside humanity. This "position outside of nations", of which the Pentateuch speaks, is realized in the concept of Israel and its particularism. It is a particularism that conditions universality, and it is a moral category rather than a historical fact to do with Israel, even if the historical Israel has in fact been faithful to the concept of Israel and, on the subject of morality, felt responsibilities and obligations which it demands of no one, but which sustain the world.[46]

Appendix A.
The Concept of Plausibility

I have used the term *plausible* to characterize valid interpretations of Romans. But it is an axiom of historical demonstration that one must produce probable, not merely "plausible," accounts of the past.[1] This axiom has been carried over into the historical-critical interpretation of texts, E. D. Hirsch being one of its most insistent advocates.[2]

In the Western philosophical tradition, the attack on plausibility begins with Plato, who charged the rhetoricians with preferring plausibility (*credibilia*) to truth (*Phaedrus* 267). Quintilian, after quoting Plato, notes that the rhetorician Cornelius Celsus defined the rhetorical goal as the "semblance of truth" (*simile veri*) (Quintilian 2.15.32). The *Rhetorica ad Herennium* (attributed to Cicero) counsels using both the true and the plausible (1.2.3), explaining that the "statement of facts will have plausibility if it answers the requirements of the usual, the expected, and the natural" (1.9.16).[3] This assertion suggests why "plausibility" is a problematic concept. The plausible is governed by public criteria, which may be critical or uncritical. Thus, for a general courtroom audience, the test of plausibility is "verisimilitude," as judged by common opinion, which may be a mere "semblance" of truth that wins applause ("plausible" derives from *plaudere*) from the credulous crowd.

Nevertheless, since probability judgments may lead one to conclude that two interpretations are more or less equally probable, the judgments "equally plausible" and "equally probable" approach equivalence. More specifically, two plausible interpretations that are critical and rigorous by probabilistic methods are equally probable interpretations. This is why one can use the expressions "most plausible" and "most probable" interchangeably. Hence we confront the oddity that in common critical parlance, the expressions "probable" and "most probable" stand opposed to "merely plausible," while "most plausible" is virtually the equivalent of "most probable."

Let me propose a definition of *rigorous* plausibility, to be distinguished from the kind of plausibility, based on permissive canons of demonstration, that Hirsch attacks. Critical plausibility designates interpretive demonstration that may produce multiple, competing interpretations, all of which are more or less equally probable. Thus the most assiduous judgments of plausibility are neither more nor less rigorous than the most assiduous judgments about what is most probable, if they depend on the same methods.

Owing to the inexact nature of interpretive judgment, "equally probable" is not a quantifiable entity and may, therefore, designate interpretations whose probability is judged differently by disparate competent interpreters. The expression "more or less equally probable" nicely conveys this latitude of rough or relative equality. The question, then, is how to define this relative equality. Usually, the interpretation that one interpreter admits as being plausible but rejects is *someone else's most probable interpretation*. I therefore suggest a rule of thumb for inclusion: where (1) one has reasonable doubt that what is deemed less probable is in fact so and (2) other competent interpreters are confident that the interpretation in question is equally or most probable in comparison with other competing interpretations, one ought to treat the interpretation in question as equally probable and number it among the valid plausible interpretations. This rule fits the definition of a text's meaning as apparent meaning. A text's probable meaning is a meaning perceived as such by interpreters, who, as a representative group operating with the appropriate public lexicon, are the only conceivable index of what a probable meaning is. To that extent, interpreters must judge plausible meaning according to their own sensibilities, taking cues from one another.

Equally probable interpretations of Romans stand for plausible representations of Paul's apparent meaning. Thus the original meaning of Romans is the set of all rigorously plausible interpretations of the text, where "plausible" denotes what competent readers, using the shared cultural-linguistic lexicon of Paul's public environment, would have been justified in construing as Paul's apparent intent.

Appendix B.
Unintended Meaning

According to E. D. Hirsch, if an interpreter imposes a meaning that is not the author's, then it is a mere accident of language if that meaning can be plausibly defended on the basis of internal and external evidence; the meaning is not in any valid sense a meaning *of the text*.[1] The theory that "linguistic signs can somehow speak their own meaning," Hirsch says, is "a mystical idea that has never been persuasively defended."[2] "Never been persuasively *explained*" might be a better way of putting this objection. Moreover, Hirsch's own discussion leaves much unaccounted for. He recognizes that by situating a literary text within any number of extratextual interpretive frameworks (i.e., by defining the genre of the text in different ways), interpreters can produce very different plausible interpretations. But having made this demonstration, he offers no explanation of how an author can produce a text that succeeds in its intended genre but at the same time is capable of making excellent sense according to other identifications of its genre. In addition, Hirsch provides no explanation of how two interpreters, operating with the same set of assumptions about the genre of a complex text, can defend competing interpretations that are equally plausible. That interpreters do just that all the time is an intriguing phenomenon. How is it possible that we are able—often, no doubt, without arriving at authorial intent—to give two contrary readings of a complex text, providing in each reading a good account of how virtually all the parts fit together into a whole and doing so by treating the parts and the whole according to the public lexicon that governed communication in the world in which the text was produced? More important, how is it that interpretation can operate according to the rules of a given language game, do reasonable justice to the parts and the whole of the text, and produce a public sense unintended by the author that is interesting and enlightening, even profound?[3]

Like Hirsch, Walter Benn Michaels and Steven Knapp reject the notion of unintended meaning, but they do so by a slightly different route.[4] They contend that unintended meaning, as a category, is both useless and absurd. To prove this, they ask whether those who believe in the possibility of accidental meaning could accept as meaningful "marks" on a beach, produced by waves, that happen to look just like the letters (and arrangement of those letters) in the first stanza of William Wordsworth's "A Slumber Did My Spirit Seal."[5] They propose that if, while we were contemplating these marks, another wave should wash up on the beach and leave in its retreat the *second* stanza of Wordsworth's poem, then we would immediately get suspicious and wonder what intelligence could be producing this writing; that is, we would abandon the theory of accidental meaning and read as if someone (perhaps the god of the sea) had intended something by the marks. Nevertheless, they contend, neither our first assumption of remarkable unintended meaning nor our new assumption of an author can possibly affect the method by which we interpret, which is always to behave as if meaning is intentional.

Knapp and Michaels's conclusion is surely correct when it comes to how we regard writings that we think stem from an author. It is for this reason that I speak of the original meaning of Romans as the "apparent" meaning of Paul. But it does not follow that an author in fact intended the apparent meaning that we discover. Nor does it follow that unless some conscious intelligence meant to communicate something by inscribing the marks on the beach, those marks are not linguistically meaningful because they are not language.[6] In any case, I doubt that any lines of Wordsworth's poem will ever wash up on a beach, but unintended semantic effects that are coherent and interesting wash up in complex texts all the time. Classical literature produced through a long traditioning process provides an especially persuasive example of the fact that, wittingly or unwittingly, we do accept unintended meaning as constitutive of at least some revered works. A rich tradition can render some semantic accidents meaningful.

The Hebrew Bible provides a case in point. As John Barton observes, the Torah

> was the adventitious product of a long and chaotic process of redaction in which originally separate sources and fragments were woven together into a shapeless collection. But no one knew that. Consequently, the Torah was read with an assumption of coherence.[7]

That assumption allowed ancient interpreters, as it now allows modern ones, to construe the Torah as a whole, one whose meaning in fact outstrips the intentions of those who produced it. This is not to deny that our modern methods of interpretation can show the Torah to be much less coherent than it appeared in ancient glosses. But we also confront a choice: not whether to use our own modern methods but whether, in using them, to read like Ralph Rader's reader or like Stanley Fish's (see chapter 1). When we read with a presumption of coherence, assigning contradiction only where there is no plausible way to avoid it (Rader's reader), then we, too, undoubtedly discover justifiable construals that were not in the minds of any who helped produce the text.

The Jewish Torah and the Christian Bible are composed of materials shaped and reshaped by many anonymous voices, in a process governed by no singular individual or collective intelligence. Even the final redactors, whether of individual biblical "books" or of the canon as a whole, do not supply any unified intelligence comparable to that of an author who intends to communicate a meaning. Hence, Brevard Childs, speaking of the semantic effects that came about when the Jewish scriptures were arranged within the Christian Bible, advises that we ought not "overemphasize the conscious theological intentionality" of those who produced the Christian canon. "Equally as significant," he insists, "is the resulting effect of these changes in the ordering on the reading of the literature even when fortuitous elements were clearly involved."[8] In a similar vein, Gerald Sheppard, in an essay on the structure of Isaiah, argues that "the incoherency, unharmonized, and uninterpreted quality of the traditions in the book may prove as provocative as any hidden motivations of redactors we might find."[9] And who is to say that some of those ancients who advocated reading various texts together as part of a canon did not recognize (and thus intend) that the result would be more meaning—a surplus of meaning, which no one could conceive in advance of discovering?

It is also important to emphasize that the kinds of meaning produced "by accident" are of very different sorts. Some may be trifling, others momentous. Some may be complex semantic effects, others relatively isolated and simple ones. The most interesting are those effects that are significant and complex. But for obvious reasons, it is often impossible to distinguish between products of intent and products of fortuity. Yet many conflicts of interpretation are proof that significant unintended meanings do arise.

Let me give an example, drawn from the debate about the meaning of "Israel" in Romans. If a plausible argument can establish the reasonable possibility that Paul meant the church when he wrote that "all Israel" will be saved, then to admit that this is *possible* is simultaneously to admit that one of the plausible alternative interpretations—namely, that "all Israel" means the Jewish nation as a whole—could have arisen through an accident of ambiguity. For the immediate purposes of my illustration, it is not necessary to establish which interpretation is more probable, but, for the sake of argument, I will stipulate that the most probable interpretation is the one that identifies "all Israel" with the Jewish nation as a whole. In that case, the alternative interpretation ("all Israel" means the church) is merely possible. But granting this mere possibility admits a great deal. When one judges a highly unlikely interpretation to be possible, one is assuming that, from time to time, linguistic events occur in which a meaning actually *intended* by an author looks highly unlikely in comparison to an ostensible meaning that the author did *not* intend.

Moreover, the thesis that "all Israel" means the Jewish nation permits and facilitates a reading of Romans that is reasonably coherent, as well as complex and very meaningful. Thus to admit simultaneously (1) the mere possibility that Paul did not mean the whole nation of Israel in Rom. 11:26 but had the church in mind and (2) that a coherent and theologically significant (as opposed to trivial) interpretation can be defended nonetheless by construing "all Israel" as the nation is to admit, by logical implication, that a complex, coherent, and significant (by some accounts even profound) semantic effect can arise that does not originate in an author's intention and, in view of its complexity (which in this kind of example can hardly be called forced or artificial), cannot be reasonably attributed to the sheer ingenuity of an interpreter—even if it takes an interpreter to put together the pieces that bring this meaning to light.

Appendix C.
Hermeneutical Election and the
Shadow Side of the Canon

A moral approach to canonical interpretation must confront the question of ideology in the text of scripture. One important criticism that has been leveled against the canonical program advocated by Brevard Childs is that it appears to rule out ideological critique of the Bible while discounting precanonical voices that may have resisted oppressive ideologies at work in the so-called canonical process.[1]

Childs observes a generalizing tendency in the canonical process that effaces many traces of historical particularity and gives the various canonical voices the power to speak theologically across time. Accordingly, the canonical interpreter, in faithfulness to this generalizing impulse of the canon, "strives critically to discern from its kerygmatic witness a way to God which overcomes the historical moorings of both text and reader."[2] There is, however, a crucial difference between a canonical rhetoric addressing a universal audience (the church universal and the world) and the actual ability of any text to speak across cultures and across the gaps between one historically circumscribed knowledge system (*epistemê*) and another.

What Childs describes as the largely generalized shape of the canonical witness is, sociohistorically speaking, a witness shaped at a general ideological level. We can describe general ideological systems of the ancient Mediterranean world that existed across many centuries, some of which have been more generally pervasive in human history. The generalized voice of the canon may reflect an erasure of many of the particular political purposes and motives at work in the precanonical history of its writings and traditions, but it is not for that reason free of the ideologies that may have influenced the canonical process itself or of the ideologies belonging to the larger knowledge system in which the canon was formed.[3]

Frank Kermode has described the remarkable power of a "classic" to speak across the discontinuities and ruptures of history and culture.[4] A sacred canon with the power of a classic is capacitated to transmit and recommend to all not only its humanizing ideologies, its liberating visions of human life in God's world, but also whatever dehumanizing ideologies it bears and, in effect, stamps with a divine imprimatur.[5] Therefore canonical criticism ought to include ideological critique of the Christian Bible.

Ideological critique of the canon would produce the *shadow side* of the canon, staking out its capacity to make and keep life inhumane. But this means that not only other interpreters, making different arguments and producing their own ideological critiques of our constructive interpretation, *but also this very shadow reading itself,* along with those other plausible readings that we produce and defend through criticism, have the potential to challenge our own sense of what makes and keeps life human.

It is therefore important to distinguish between canonical *criticism,* as a descriptive and evaluative task, and what might be called canonical *jurisprudence,* which adjudicates with a view to the use of scripture by the church in accord with the purpose (*scopus*) of scripture. The task of canonical criticism would include the discrimination of the full range of plausible construals of the canonical text and a subjection of this range to whatever forms of analysis and evaluation interest interpreters. Canonical jurisprudence, for its part, would build on canonical-critical work, seeking to adjudicate among the various possibilities for reasonable construal— within a text and between texts—in accord with the purpose of scripture (and any other principles of fair and humane interpretation that such an approach may establish for itself).

Let me illustrate this for the interpretation of Romans. Today a growing number of scholars regard Paul as a witness against anti-Jewishness.[6] Moreover, the increasing tendency to construe Rom. 11:25–29 as evidence that Paul believed in the irrevocable identity of the Jewish people as true Israel can be described, from a sociological standpoint, as a piece of a larger shared interpretive agenda to combat anti-Semitism in biblical studies and Christian faith. That agenda is explicit when, speaking in the language of interpretive options, Lloyd Gaston suggests that to understand Paul as Judaism-affirming is not only possible but necessary after Auschwitz.[7] What is uncommon in Gaston's argument is the frank implication that we ought to choose one interpretation over another on the basis of ethical considerations; that we should *elect* not necessarily the most likely interpretation but the ethically most attractive one.

Gaston's argument is in part a response to Rosemary Radford Ruether's charge that the roots of anti-Semitism go back to the New Testament and are found in Paul.[8] Ruether's work would suggest that to point out what makes Paul susceptible of anti-Jewish interpretations is also necessary— especially after Auschwitz.

Pauline scholars are right to point out that because the historical Paul's critique of aspects of the Judaism he knew belonged to an intra-Jewish dialogue (Paul himself being a Jew), that critique cannot properly be characterized as "anti-Jewish." It is nevertheless legitimate to inquire whether Paul's arguments provide plausible warrants for anti-Jewish theology when Paul is construed as part of the Christian Bible, which is a later literary formation produced outside Judaism. Does the conversion of the historical Paul's letters into elements of a Christian canon create the semantic conditions in which "roots" of anti-Semitism do appear, at least in some plausible readings of (the canonical) Paul? And if so, is it wrong to elect, for theological use, a critically justifiable interpretation of the canonical Paul that has proven conducive to Christian anti-Jewishness when another justifiable interpretation is available that is not conducive to anti-Jewish theology? Or, alternately, is it wrong to choose that other viable interpretation, for the sake of carnal Israel, thereby *suppressing* those plausible ways of reading the canonical Paul that comport better with anti-Jewish theology?

To be sure, what counts as "anti-Jewish" is itself open to at least some debate, as is the question of what is conducive to anti-Jewishness. Moreover, arguments about the definition of anti-Jewishness take place not only between Jews and non-Jews (and among non-Jews talking about Jews) but also among Jews themselves. Without getting into the substance of such disputes here, I wish to make some formal observations. The historical Paul had some harsh things to say about his kinfolk. But his critique of Judaism can be regarded as an intramural struggle, within Judaism. As an ancient Jewish scholar, Paul had every right to reinterpret Judaism by his own lights and to challenge other Jews to see things from his point of view. If we see Paul's teaching as critique by an insider, then what he says can scarcely be construed as "anti-Jewish." If, however, we find evidence that Paul understood himself to have left Judaism, then the picture of the historical Paul's stance toward Jewish faith and life will assume a different quality for us.

But however we define the stance of historical Paul vis-à-vis Judaism, that Paul is not the canonical Paul. The canonical Paul belongs to a Christian Bible that assumes the separation between Christianity and Judaism. We may wish to argue that the canonical Paul, construed as bearer of the voice of the historical Paul, puts pressure within the canon on that very assumption of a separation, or that he at least challenges any anti-Jewish conception of that assumption. But we must also consider how the larger canonical context shapes the reading of Paul. As parts of a Christian and not a Jewish Bible, some of Paul's letters can be plausibly construed as having an anti-Jewish tendency, or at least some anti-Jewish implications. How ought a canonical method of interpretation treat this semantic effect? What are the ethical issues that must be taken into account in that treatment?

We may begin by inquiring after the Christian interest in proving that Paul is/was not "anti-Jewish." To argue that anti-Judaism is a dogma invented by the post-Pauline church but without any basis in Paul is to defend not only Judaism but also Christianity, at least as expressed in one of its most highly esteemed scriptural sources. It is to exonerate the Pauline fountainhead of Christian faith and pin the blame solely on *others*, obscuring the fact that early Christians found warrants for anti Judaism in Paul and did so not only by torturing the plain sense of his text but also, at least to a degree, by opting for plausible interpretations that served their own ideological interests. But by vindicating Paul without carrying out an ideological critique of the canonical Paul's textual discourse about Jews and Judaism, one risks simply reinforcing the centuries-long presumption of the church that Christians can simply trust the descriptions of Jews and Judaism that they find in Paul's letters—at least when those letters are fairly interpreted by impartial scholars. We ought to bear in mind that many past Christian interpreters whose discourse about Jews and Judaism now appears to us to contain anti-Jewish content did not regard themselves as anti-Jewish and in some cases saw themselves as defenders of the Jewish people. The question of anti-Jewishness in the canonical Paul must therefore be kept open. As definitions of anti-Jewishness change, fresh analysis of the semantic potential of Paul's text is required.

Keeping this question open does not preclude making interpretive judgments based on our best understanding. Most important, the question of anti-Jewishness in the *canonical* Paul ought not be kept radically open when we interpret Romans as scripture. A canonical approach requires that we make judgments about how to construe the canonical Paul's ambiguous rhetoric.

At the same time, canonical adjudication requires acknowledging the shadow side of the canon in those plausible construals that we reject as inappropriate to the use of the Bible as scripture. Thus ideological critique has an important place in canonical interpretation, without becoming the last word.

Notes

Introduction

1. See John Sandys-Wunsch and Laurence Eldridge, "J. P. Gabler and the Distinction between Biblical and Dogmatic Theology: Translation, Commentary, and Discussion of His Originality," *Scottish Journal of Theology* 33 (1980): 145.

2. On this distinction, applied to the Book of Isaiah, see Gerald T. Sheppard, "The Book of Isaiah: Competing Structures according to a Late Modern Description of Its Shape and Scope," in *Society of Biblical Literature 1992 Seminar Papers*, ed. Eugene H. Lovering (Atlanta: Scholars Press, 1992), 554–69.

Chapter 1.
Elusive Israel

1. See Alan F. Segal's framing of these two questions in "Paul's Experience and Romans 9–11," *Princeton Seminary Bulletin*, supplementary issue, no. 1 (1990): 57–58; also idem, *Paul the Convert: The Apostolate and Apostasy of Saul the Pharisee* (New Haven, Conn.: Yale University Press, 1990), 276–77.

2. Commenting as a literary theorist about the critical reviews that his novels have received, Umberto Eco acknowledges that in some cases he can respond only by saying, "No, I did not mean this, but I must agree that the text says it." See his *Interpretation and Overinterpretation*, with Richard Rorty, Jonathan Culler, and Christine Brooke-Rose, ed. Stefan Collini (Cambridge: Cambridge University Press, 1992), 73.

3. For a somewhat similar conception, see Jerrold Levinson's notion of "hypothetical intent" in his essay "Intention and Interpretation: A Last Look," in *Intention and Interpretation*, ed. Gary Iseminger (Philadelphia: Temple University Press, 1992), 221–56.

4. Brevard S. Childs, *The New Testament as Canon: An Introduction* (Philadelphia: Fortress Press, 1984), 24–27; idem, *Biblical Theology of the Old and New Testaments: Theological Reflection on the Christian Bible* (Minneapolis: Fortress Press, 1992), 70–71.

5. I do not pretend to know when this first occurred or if there were debates about it. We know from Justin Martyr that by the middle of the second century, it was customary in Rome to read apostolic writings along with the Prophets in

Sunday worship (*1 Apology* 67.3). I am imagining the practice occurring at an earlier date simply as a way of joining conceptually the historical meaning of Romans with the use of Romans as an authoritative text. This does not require thinking of Romans as being on a par with the (Jewish) scriptures. That equality clearly did not happen until later, and I doubt that Justin himself accorded scriptural status to any of the apostolic writings. See Charles H. Cosgrove, "Justin Martyr and the Emerging Christian Canon: Observations on the Purpose and Destination of the Dialogue with Trypho," *Vigiliae Christianae* 36 (1982): 209–32.

6. For a transcript of a debate among modern scholars concerning Paul's teaching about Israel in Romans 9—11, see Werner Georg Kümmel, "Die Probleme von Römer 9–11 in der gegenwärtigen Forschungslage," in *Die Israelfrage nach Röm 9–11*, ed. Lorenzo De Lorenzi (Rome: St. Paul vor den Mauern, 1977), 34–56.

7. In making all three debate partners male, I do not mean to assume that a woman in the Roman church could not have held her own with the men. I am simply trying to reflect the cultural fact that, in Paul's context, it was men who were socialized to be thinkers and interpreters of scripture. It also seemed simpler to avoid the burden of doing justice to the gender dynamics that would have been present in a mixed trio—dynamics that I do not feel competent to render for the ancient context, and which, in any case, lie beyond my scope. For the same considerations of historical faithfulness, I have my three readers use masculine language in referring to the Deity, as I also do when characterizing Paul's views.

8. In an earlier effort, I sought to imagine how a Jewish reader who was highly suspicious of Paul might have heard Romans 1—4 and been conditioned thereby to make interpretive judgments about the remainder of the letter. See Charles H. Cosgrove, "The Justification of the Other: An Interpretation of Rom. 1:18–4:25," in *Society of Biblical Literature 1992 Seminar Papers*, ed. Eugene H. Lovering (Atlanta: Scholars Press, 1992), 613–34. In addition to the narrower focus of that essay (concentrated on Romans 1—4), it differs from the imaginary dialogue I construct here in that in "The Justification of the Other" I treated Romans as a speech, heard once in its rhetorical unfolding (when first read to the Roman Christians), whereas here I am regarding Romans as a text to be read and reread.

9. Jouette M. Bassler, *Divine Impartiality: Paul and a Theological Axiom* (Society of Biblical Literature Dissertation Series 59; Chico, Calif.: Scholars Press, 1982), 185.

10. What makes Paul's application of the Jewish teaching about God's impartiality so provocative is not simply that he applies it to God's dealings with Jews and gentiles but that he combines it with his own axiom "There is no distinction" (Rom. 3:22; 10:12).

11. John J. Collins, *Between Athens and Jerusalem: Jewish Identity in the Hellenistic Diaspora* (New York: Crossroad, 1983), 137–74.

12. Thomas R. Schreiner, "Paul and Perfect Obedience to the Law: An Evaluation of the View of E. P. Sanders," *Westminster Theological Journal* 47 (1985): 260–61.

13. Stanley K. Stowers has argued that the prophetic critique in Rom. 2:17ff. is

aimed at a particular type of Jewish teacher and not in any wholesale way against Jews; see chaps. 4 and 5 of his *A Rereading of Romans: Justice, Jews, and Gentiles* (New Haven, Conn.: Yale University Press, 1994).

14. For expressions of this idea in Second Temple Judaism, see, for example, *T. Levi* 15.4 and *T. Asher* 7.7.

15. I have constructed this speech by Reuben in accord with certain elements of Stanley Stowers's interpretation of Romans (*A Rereading of Romans*, 1–125).

16. Louis Finkelstein, as quoted in E. P. Sanders, *Paul and Palestinian Judaism: A Comparison of Patterns of Religion* (Philadelphia: Fortress Press, 1977), 148–49.

17. See James D. G. Dunn, *Romans 9—16* (Word Biblical Commentary 38B; Dallas: Word Books, 1988), 689 and 696–97; M. Eugene Boring, "The Language of Universal Salvation in Paul," *Journal of Biblical Literature* 105 (1986): 269–92.

18. See Heikki Räisänen, "Paul, God, and Israel—Romans 9–11 in Recent Research," in *The Social World of Formative Christianity and Judaism: Essays in Tribute to Howard Clark Kee*, ed. Jacob Neusner et al. (Philadelphia: Fortress Press, 1988), 178–206.

19. N. T. Wright, *The Climax of the Covenant: Christ and the Law in Pauline Theology* (Edinburgh: T. & T. Clark, 1991; Minneapolis: Fortress Press, 1992), 232–51; Hervé Ponsot, "Et ainsi tout Israel sera sauvé: Rom., XI, 26a," *Revue biblique* 89 (1982): 406–17.

20. E.g., Paul W. Meyer, "Romans," in *Harper's Bible Commentary*, ed. James L. Mays (San Francisco: Harper & Row, 1988), 1155–56.

21. Dunn, *Romans 9—16*, 681–82.

22. Ibid., 540.

23. J. Christiaan Beker, "Romans 9–11 in the Context of the Early Church," *Princeton Seminary Bulletin*, supplementary issue, no. 1 (1990): 45–47; cf. Räisänen, "Paul, God, and Israel."

24. James D. G. Dunn, *Romans 1—8* (Word Biblical Commentary 38A; Dallas: Word Books, 1988), 124–25.

25. See Walter Schmithals, *Der Römerbrief: Ein Kommentar* (Gütersloh: Gütersloher Verlagshaus Gerd Mohn, 1988), 398, 403–4.

26. See, e.g., 1QS 5; see also chapter 2, n. 32 below; Otfried Hofius, "Das Evangelium und Israel: Erwägungen zu Römer 9–11," *Zeitschrift für Theologie und Kirche* 83 (1986): 305; Johann Maier and Kurt Schubert, *Die Qumran-Essener: Texte der Schriftrollen und Lebensbild der Gemeinde* (Munich and Basel: Ernst Reinhardt Verlag, 1982), chap. 9 (esp. 73–75). See further the reflection of the "elect number" theory in Rev. 7:4–8. This is probably the true Israel made up of Christians (Rev. 14:1–5). They have assumed the identity and rights of Israel and are distinguished from those "who say that they are Jews and are not but are a synagogue of Satan" (Rev. 2:9; cf. 3:9).

27. See Klyne R. Snodgrass, "Justification by Grace—To the Doers: An Analysis of the Place of Romans 2 in the Theology of Paul," *New Testament Studies* 32 (1986): 81.

28. On this way of construing Romans 4, see Cosgrove, "Justification of the

Other," 628–31; Hendrikus Boers, *The Justification of the Gentiles: Paul's Letters to the Galatians and the Romans* (Peabody, Mass.: Hendrickson Publishers, 1994), 181 83.

29. See Nils Alstrup Dahl, "The Doctrine of Justification: Its Social Function and Implications," in *Studies in Paul: Theology for the Early Christian Mission* (Minneapolis: Augsburg Publishing House, 1977), 80.

30. Cf. Richard B. Hays, *Echoes of Scripture in the Letters of Paul* (New Haven, Conn.: Yale University Press, 1989), 47.

31. See further Charles H. Cosgrove, "What If Some Have Not Believed? The Occasion and Thrust of Romans 3 1–8," *Zeitschrift für die neutestamentliche Wissenschaft* 78 (1987): 90–105.

32. Thus Dunn, *Romans 9—16*, 679.

33. Reuben is correct. Even in 2:28–29, Paul does not qualify the name Jew with adjectives such as *true* or *false*. But Paul's argument in this passage has suggested to many interpreters that this is what the text means. The RSV has "real Jew" in v. 28; the NRSV drops "real."

34. Reuben's view has been argued perhaps no more persuasively in recent scholarship than by Richard B. Hays, "ΠΙΣΤΙΣ and Pauline Christology: What Is at Stake?" in *Society of Biblical Literature 1991 Seminar Papers*, ed. Eugene H. Lovering (Atlanta: Scholars Press, 1991), 30:714–29; idem, *The Faith of Jesus Christ: An Investigation of the Narrative Substructure of Galatians 3:1–4:11* (Society of Biblical Literature Dissertation Series 56; Chico, Calif.: Scholars Press, 1983). The traditionally dominant view, represented by Chariton and Simeon, has been most effectively argued of late by James D. G. Dunn, "Once More, ΠΙΣΤΙΣ ΧΡΙΣΤΟΥ," in *Society of Biblical Literature 1991 Seminar Papers*, ed. Eugene H. Lovering (Atlanta: Scholars Press, 1991), 30:730–44.

35. On the use of rhetorical "suspense" in Romans 9—11, see chapter 2, below.

36. James R. Kincaid, "Coherent Readers, Incoherent Texts," *Critical Inquiry* 3 (1976–77): 781–802.

37. Ralph Rader, as quoted in ibid., 786.

38. Ralph Rader, as quoted in ibid., 788.

39. Ibid., 790.

40. Ibid., 794–802.

41. See, further, chapter 2, below.

42. Räisänen, "Paul, God, and Israel."

43. E. Elizabeth Johnson, "Romans 9–11: The Faithfulness and Impartiality of God," in *Pauline Theology*, vol. 3: *Romans*, ed. David M. Hay and E. Elizabeth Johnson (Minneapolis: Fortress Press, 1995), 222.

44. Ibid.

45. Timothy Bahti, "Ambiguity and Indeterminacy: The Juncture," *Comparative Literature* 38 (1986): 209–23.

46. Ibid., 213

47. Ibid., 212–13.

48. On the meaning of "rigorously plausible," see Appendix A, below.

Chapter 2.
Hermeneutical Election

1. Frank Kermode, *The Genesis of Secrecy: On the Interpretation of Narrative* (Cambridge, Mass.: Harvard University Press, 1979), 72.

2. Giovanni Battista Montini [Pope Paul VI], as quoted in Hans Küng, *Infallible? An Unresolved Inquiry,* expanded ed. (New York: Continuum, 1994), 36.

3. E.g., K. L. Schmidt, *Die Judenfrage im Lichte der Kapitel 9–11 des Römerbriefes* (Theologische Studien 13; Zurich: Evangelischer-Verlag, 1943), 29.

4. Cf. John Piper, *The Justification of God: An Exegetical and Theological Study of Romans 9:1–23* (Grand Rapids: Baker Book House, 1983), 163–99. Piper makes a strong exegetical case that while Paul's argument focuses on the question of Israel and God's interaction with peoples in history, it establishes, as one of its premises, that God unconditionally elects individuals to eternal glory or eternal destruction, the election to wrath serving the election to mercy. Piper's study is, to a significant degree, concerned with explicating this premise and its logic.

5. C. H. Dodd, *The Epistle of Paul to the Romans* (London: Hodder & Stoughton, 1932), 159.

6. James D. G. Dunn, *Romans 9—16* (Word Biblical Commentary 38B; Dallas: Word Books, 1988), 559–60.

7. Recall the discussion of this point in chapter 1.

8. Jouette Bassler's illuminating study of the Jewish principle of divine impartiality and its function in Romans strengthens the impression that God's undifferentiating treatment of Jews and gentiles is a central point of the letter. See Jouette M. Bassler, "Divine Impartiality in Paul's Letter to the Romans," *Novum Testamentum* 26 (1984): 43–58; idem, *Divine Impartiality: Paul and a Theological Axiom* (Society of Biblical Literature Dissertation Series 59; Chico, Calif.: Scholars Press, 1982).

9. See, e.g., J. Christiaan Beker, *Paul the Apostle: The Triumph of God in Life and Thought,* 2d ed. (Philadelphia: Fortress Press, 1984), 331–37.

10. J. Christiaan Beker, "Romans 9–11 in the Context of the Early Church," *Princeton Seminary Bulletin,* supplementary issue, no. 1 (1990): 45–47; Heikki Räisänen, "Paul, God, and Israel—Romans 9–11 in Recent Research," in *The Social World of Formative Christianity and Judaism: Essays in Tribute to Howard Clark Kee,* ed. Jacob Neusner et al. (Philadelphia: Fortress Press, 1988).

11. E. Elizabeth Johnson, *The Function of Apocalyptic and Wisdom Traditions in Romans 9—11* (Society of Biblical Literature Dissertation Series 109; Atlanta: Scholars Press, 1989), 175.

12. In his book *The Justification of the Gentiles: Paul's Letters to the Galatians and the Romans* (Peabody, Mass.: Hendrickson Publishers, 1994), Hendrikus Boers discovers such a unity in the "deep structure" of Paul's thinking.

13. Richard B. Hays, *Echoes of Scripture in the Letters of Paul* (New Haven, Conn.: Yale University Press, 1989), 46.

14. John Hollander, *The Figure of the Echo: A Mode of Allusion in Milton and Af-ter* (Berkeley. University of California Press, 1981).

15. Hays, *Echoes of Scripture*, 20.

16. Paul's quotation from Hos. 2:23 in Rom. 9:25 does not quite conform to the Hebrew text or to the Septuagint. Paul's quotation from Hosea in Rom. 9:26 is found at Hos. 1:10 in the Septuagint and at 2:1 in the Hebrew.

17. Wayne A. Meeks, "On Trusting an Unpredictable God: A Hermeneutical Meditation on Romans 9–11," in *Faith and History: Essays in Honor of Paul W. Meyer*, ed. John T. Carroll et al. (Atlanta: Scholars Press, 1990), 111–18.

18. Ibid., 118 (see also 112–13).

19. Ibid., 110.

20. Ibid., 108.

21. According to Aristotle, anagnorisis is best when it occurs with a peripeteia (*Poetics* 11).

22. N. T. Wright, *The Climax of the Covenant: Christ and the Law in Pauline The-ology* (Edinburgh: T. & T. Clark, 1991; Minneapolis: Fortress Press, 1992), 246–51; see also Hervé Ponsot, "Et ainsi tout Israel sera sauvé: Rom., XI, 26a," *Revue biblique* 89 (1982): 406–17.

23. François Refoulé, ". . . *Et ainsi tout Israël sera sauvé*": *Romains 11:25–32* (Paris: Cerf, 1984).

24. In Rom. 3:1–20, Paul lumps the Jewish people as a whole together with the gentiles as a mass of the damned. This is a difficult passage to interpret, especially as it unfolds in vv. 1–8. One thing seems clear to me: Rom. 3:1–8 makes the point that God is not unjust to inflict wrath on Israel, which implies that this is exactly and finally what God will do (or is already doing; cf. 1:18, 24, 26). Paul's affirmation that God must be true, though every human being is false, in no way relieves this bleak picture, since God's truth is vindicated, according to the argument of this passage, precisely in executing judgment and inflicting wrath, not in showing mercy.

25. Cf. N. T. Wright's cautions against making Rom. 11:25–27 a starting point for interpreting Romans 9—11 as a whole, rather than according the whole, from the beginning of the letter through 11:24, decisive weight in deciding how to understand 11:25–27 (*Climax of the Covenant*, 246–47).

26. In *De Oratore* 3.204, Cicero includes *communicatio* in a list of rhetorical devices. Quintilian reproduces this list verbatim in *Institutio Oratoria* 9.1.30 and elaborates on *communicatio* in 9.2.20. The equivalent term in Greek rhetoric is ἀνακοίνωσις.

27. Ch. Perelman and L. Olbrechts-Tyteca, *The New Rhetoric: A Treatise on Argumentation*, trans. John Wilkinson and Purcell Weaver (Notre Dame, Ind.: University of Notre Dame Press, 1969).

28. Ibid., 493.

29. Ibid., 494.

30. Heinrich Lausberg, *Handbuch der literarischen Rhetorik: Eine Grundlegung der*

Wissenschaft, 2d ed., 2 vols. (Munich: Max Hueber, 1960). The term *sustentatio* does not appear in the Latin section of Lausberg's index. In the French index, the terms *suspens, suspense*, and *suspension* appear. The reader is referred to the chapters on poetics and also to discussions in the chapters on rhetoric that treat matters involving various kinds of "suspension" but not the rhetorical figure described by Quintilian.

31. Verres, Cicero discloses, set free the band of slave conspirators who had already been convicted and then sentenced by Verres himself. The shameful profit Verres no doubt extorted in this case pales, Cicero says, in comparison with the dishonor of setting loose "slaves condemned for a crime that endangered the lives of all free men" (*Against Verres* 2.5.6[13]; *The Verrine Orations*, trans. L. H. G. Greenwood, rev. ed. [Loeb Classical Library; Cambridge, Mass.: Harvard University Press, 1935; London: William Heinemann, 1935], vol. 2). Cicero, and no doubt his audience, found this betrayal of the public trust "monstrous."

32. E. P. Sanders suspects that a similar idea prevailed at Qumran, expressed in 1QH 6,7ff. The full number of the elect is to be completed not by the salvation of all Israel but by the incorporation of other survivors who belong to the eschatological elect. See E. P. Sanders, *Paul and Palestinian Judaism: A Comparison of Patterns of Religion* (Philadelphia: Fortress Press, 1977), 250. On the idea of an elect remnant that is not preserved for the sake of Israel as a whole, see chapter 1, n. 26, above.

33. The first of these interpretations is defended by Refoulé, "... *Et ainsi tout Israël sera sauvé,*" 142–43; the second is argued by Ponsot, "Et ainsi tout Israel sera sauvé."

34. Cf. Ernst Käsemann: "Der Satz bricht jäh ab. Er springt aus dem Felde scheinbar abstrakter Möglichkeiten und, wie es sogar in 22f. noch aussieht, hypothetischer Erwägungen in die Realität. . . . Er tut es allerdings so, dass jetzt heraustritt, in Wahrheit seien die Möglichkeiten nicht abstrakt, die Erwägungen nicht hypothetisch gewesen. . . . Gottes Recht hat ein konkretes Ziel" (*An die Römer*, 4th ed. [Handbuch zum Neuen Testament 8a; Tübingen: J. C. B. Mohr (Paul Siebeck), 1980], 263). C. K. Barrett doubts that Paul speaks hypothetically even for a moment: "The construction is rhetorical in style, 'What if this is so?' being used for 'Why should this not be so?'; that is, 'This is in fact so, and there is no reason why it should not be so'" (*A Commentary on Paul's Epistle to the Romans*, Harper's New Testament Commentaries [New York: Harper & Brothers, 1957], 189).

35. For a discussion of the way in which "performative speech" entails a "logic of self-involvement," see Donald Evans, *The Logic of Self-Involvement* (New York: Herder & Herder, 1968).

36. On the whole debate over the "new" ethnography as it emerged in cultural anthropology in the 1960s, see Pertti J. Pelto, *Anthropological Research: The Structure of Inquiry* (New York: Harper & Row, 1970). The parallel movement in sociology was signaled by Peter Winch's book *The Idea of a Social Science and Its Relation to Philosophy* (London: Routledge & Kegan Paul, 1958).

37. The famous expression "the willing suspension of disbelief" derives from

Samuel Taylor Coleridge, *Biographia Literaria or Biographical Sketches of My Literary Life and Opinions,* ed. John Calvin Metcalf (New York: Macmillan Co., 1926), 191 (chap. 14).

38. Brevard Childs has recently revived the "rule of faith" by advocating its use in canonical interpretation; see his *Biblical Theology of the Old and New Testaments: Theological Reflections on the Christian Bible* (Minneapolis: Fortress Press, 1992), 67–68.

39. There are, however, strong forms of ethnomethodology that require an analogue to the assumptions of a sacred hermeneutic by demanding that the ethnographer so join the community to be understood as effectively to surrender his or her own cultural identity and become a genuine insider.

40. For a discussion of this point, see Appendix B.

41. Umberto Eco, *The Limits of Interpretation* (Bloomington: Indiana University Press, 1990), 6, 27–43, 140–49; cf. idem, *Interpretation and Overinterpretation,* with Richard Rorty, Jonathan Culler, and Christine Brooke-Rose, ed. Stefan Collini (Cambridge: Cambridge University Press, 1992), 45–66.

42. David Lehman, *Signs of the Times: Deconstruction and the Fall of Paul de Man* (New York: Poseidon Press, 1991), 77. Nevertheless, deconstruction also poses as a revolutionary movement. The inner logic of the paradox that deconstruction could be both revolutionary and nihilistic is suggested by Terry Eagleton's observation that deconstruction is a risk-free form of subversiveness: "Unable to break the structures of state power, post-structuralism found it possible instead to subvert the structures of language." "Nobody," Eagleton wryly comments, "was likely to beat you over the head for doing so" (*Literary Theory: An Introduction* [Minneapolis: University of Minnesota Press, 1983], 142).

43. Fredric Jameson, *The Political Unconscious: Narrative as a Socially Symbolic Act* (Ithaca, N.Y.: Cornell University Press, 1981), 31–32.

44. The term *ideology* is used in many different senses. I do not adhere to the classical Marxist sense but define ideology as a conceptual framework (see Thomas S. Kuhn, *The Copernican Revolution: Planetary Astronomy in the History of Western Thought* [Cambridge, Mass.: Harvard University Press, 1957], 36–39) regarded from the standpoint of its self-serving aspects, whether those be the interests of an individual or of a group. In any given social situation competing ideologies may exist, and not only one "ruling" ideology. On the history of the word *ideology* and its use as a modern critical concept, see Jorge Larrain, *The Concept of Ideology* (Athens: University of Georgia Press, 1979).

45. Juan Luis Segundo, "The Hermeneutic Circle," in *Liberation of Theology,* trans. John Drury (Maryknoll, N.Y.: Orbis Books, 1976), 7–38. Latin American liberation theology as a whole is a self-conscious challenge to the prevailing tendency to regard the interest of the interpreter as an unavoidable factor nevertheless to be resisted as far as possible. Segundo presents one such liberationist challenge in the form of a theory of scriptural hermeneutics. And as Segundo points out, the black liberation theology of James Cone also entails a hermeneutic in

which a decision for the liberation of black people is self-consciously adopted as a hermeneutical norm governing theological construction. See also the excellent treatment of the role of ethics and moral formation in interpretation by Stephen E. Fowl and L. Gregory Jones, *Reading in Communion: Scripture and Ethics in Christian Life* (Grand Rapids: Wm. B. Eerdmans Publishing Co., 1991).

46. Segundo, "Hermeneutic Circle," 10.

47. Rudolf Bultmann, "Is Exegesis without Presuppositions Possible?" in *Existence and Faith: Shorter Writings of Rudolf Bultmann*, selected, translated, and introduced by Schubert M. Ogden (Cleveland and New York: World Publishing Co., 1960), 289–96.

48. Bultmann, too, thought of a "life relation" to the subject matter of the text enabling understanding. In the experience of revelation, that preunderstanding, according to Bultmann, is not modified by being given a new content but is rather "radicalized." See Rudolf Bultmann, "The Concept of Revelation in the New Testament," in *Existence and Faith*, 60–62, 85–90.

49. Juan Luis Segundo, "Ideologies and Faith," in *Liberation of Theology*, trans. Drury, 100–101.

50. Ibid., 101.

51. Robin Scroggs, "The New Testament and Ethics: How Do We Get from There to Here?" in *Perspectives on the New Testament: Essays in Honor of Frank Stagg*, ed. Charles H. Talbert (Macon, Ga.: Mercer University Press, 1985).

52. This is Leopold von Ranke's oft-quoted phrase ("wie es eigentlich gewesen") from the introduction to his history of the Latin and Germanic peoples (1824). For a discussion, see Hajo Holborn, "The Science of History," in *History and the Humanities* (Garden City, N.Y.: Doubleday & Co., 1972), 81–97.

53. E. Allan Farnsworth, *Contracts*, 2d ed. (Boston: Little, Brown & Co., 1990), 511 (sec. 7.9).

54. Ibid.

55. Umberto Eco has suggested that we imagine authors, readers, and texts themselves as having their own respective "intentions" and "rights." See Eco, *Interpretation and Overinterpretation*, 23–25. Eco, however, has in view the way in which such intentions and rights compete within a given conception of the text. My focus is on how different conceptions of the text (corresponding to different uses) eliminate or at least diminish competitions between these "rights."

56. For discussions and descriptions of canonical interpretation, see Brevard S. Childs, *The Old Testament as Scripture: An Introduction* (Philadelphia: Fortress Press, 1979); idem, *The New Testament as Canon: An Introduction* (Philadelphia: Fortress Press, 1984); idem, *Biblical Theology*; Gerald T. Sheppard, "Canonization: Hearing the Voice of the Same God through Historically Dissimilar Traditions," *Interpretation* 34 (1982): 21–33; Mark G. Brett, *Biblical Criticism in Crisis? The Impact of the Canonical Approach on Old Testament Studies* (Cambridge: Cambridge University Press, 1991); Robert W. Wall and Eugene E. Lemcio, *The New Testament as Canon: A Reader in Canonical Criticism* (Journal for the Study of the New

Testament Supplement Series 76; Sheffield: JSOT Press, 1992); Rolf Rendtorff, *Canon and Theology. Overtures to an Old Testament Theology,* trans. and ed. Margaret Kohl (Minneapolis: Fortress Press, 1993); idem, "Canonical Interpretation: A New Approach to Biblical Texts." *Pro Ecclesia* 3 (1994): 141–51; and Charles J. Scalise, *Hermeneutics as Theological Prolegomena: A Canonical Approach* (Macon, Ga.: Mercer University Press, 1994).

57. Charles M. Wood, *The Formation of Christian Understanding: Theological Hermeneutics* (Valley Forge, Penn.: Trinity Press International, 1993), 93.

58. Gerald T. Sheppard, "The Book of Isaiah: Competing Structures according to a Late Modern Description of Its Shape and Scope," in *Society of Biblical Literature 1992 Seminar Papers,* ed. Eugene H. Lovering (Atlanta: Scholars Press, 1992), 581. Because Sheppard is speaking of the canonical structure of Isaiah, he uses the term *Torah,* where he might otherwise have said "gospel" (or "faith" or "God").

59. Compare Emilio Betti's distinction between three types of interpretation corresponding to three different kinds of texts: "re-cognitive," applicable to historical and literary texts; "presentational," appropriate to dramatic and musical texts, and "normative," suited to legal and sacred texts (*Teoria generale della interpretazione* [Milan: Giuffrè, 1955], 1:347–49).

60. Richard A. Posner, *Overcoming Law* (Cambridge, Mass.: Harvard University Press, 1995), 233. For the antecedents of this view, see Benjamin N. Cardozo's classic study, *The Nature of the Judicial Process* (New Haven, Conn.: Yale University Press, 1921).

61. *Institutio Oratoria of Quintilian,* trans. H. E. Butler (Loeb Classical Library; Cambridge, Mass.: Harvard University Press, 1921; London: William Heinemann, 1921), 3:161.

62. *Scopus* is an old hermeneutical concept stemming from the post-Reformation period of Protestant biblical interpretation, with antecedents in patristic interpretation of scripture. Gerald Sheppard has recently discussed the role of "scope" in William Perkins's seventeenth-century commentary on Galatians. Perkins expounds "by the analogie of faith, by the words, scope, and circumstances of place" (as quoted by Gerald T. Sheppard, "Between Reformation and Modern Commentary: The Perception of the Scope of Biblical Books," in William Perkins, *A Commentary on Galatians,* ed. Gerald T. Sheppard [The Pilgrim Classic Commentaries; New York: Pilgrim Press, 1989], lxii). Scope refers to the purpose of the text, signifying, positively, the text's animating spirit and, negatively, a delimitation. It is at once aim and focus.

63. See Terence L. Donaldson, "The Law That Hangs (Matthew 22:40): Rabbinic Formulation and Matthean Social World," *Catholic Biblical Quarterly* 57 (1995): 689–709; Klyne R. Snodgrass, "Matthew's Understanding of the Law," *Interpretation* 46 (1992): 368–78.

64. Cf. Wolfgang Schrage, who has made a forceful case for seeing the love commandment in Matthew as the fundamental principle for right interpretation of the law in *The Ethics of the New Testament,* trans. David E. Green (Philadelphia:

Fortress Press, 1988), 148–50. See also the fine discussion in Thomas W. Ogletree, *The Use of the Bible in Christian Ethics: A Constructive Essay* (Philadelphia: Fortress Press, 1983), 104–16.

65. As far as I have been able to ascertain, this expression, which is a leitmotiv of Lehmann's life corpus, appears for the first time in the published Spanish version of an address given at Instituto Superior Evangélico de Estúdios Teológicos (ISEDET) in Buenos Aires during the early years of Latin American liberation theology. See Paul Lehmann, "¿Que está haciendo Dios en el mundo?" *Cuadernos teológicos* 10 (1961): 243–68.

66. Herein lies the kernel of truth in Bultmann's overstatement that Paul requires for the moral life of his churches "nothing that the judgment of pagans would not also recognize as good" (Rudolf Bultmann, "Das Problem der Ethik bei Paulus," *Zeitschrift für die neutestamentliche Wissenschaft* 23 [1924]: 138). Or as Wayne Meeks notes, in at least much of the rhetoric of New Testament exhortation, it is taken for granted that readers know what is right and good. Certainly some of this assumed knowledge belongs, as Meeks suggests, to common Hellenistic and Hellenistic-Jewish ethics. See Wayne A. Meeks, "Understanding Early Christian Ethics," *Journal of Biblical Literature* 105 (1986): 3–11; also idem, *The Moral World of the First Christians* (Philadelphia: Westminster Press, 1986).

67. I think what I am saying here complements the general argument of Fowl and Jones (*Reading in Communion*) about the role that character formation in community ought to play in the interpretation of scripture.

Chapter 3.
Prophetic Paul

1. E. F. Ströter, "The Second Coming of Christ in Relation to Israel," reprinted in *The Prophecy Conference Movement*, vol. 2: *Addresses on the Second Coming of the Lord Delivered at the Prophetic Conference, Allegheny, Pa., December 3–6, 1895*, bound with *Prophetic Studies of the International Prophetic Conference, Chicago, November, 1886*, ed. Donald W. Dayton (Fundamentalism in American Religion 1880–1950; New York: Garland, 1988), 148.

2. Quoted in Martin Stöhr, "Learning Step by Step in the Jewish-Christian Dialogue," *Immanuel* 24/25 (1990): 277.

3. These remarks, from an address by Martin Buber to a group of Dutch pastors, are quoted by Reinhold Niebuhr, "Martin Buber: 1878–1965," *Christianity and Crisis* 25 (July 12, 1965): 146.

4. Rosemary Radford Ruether, "Theological Anti-Semitism in the New Testament," *Christian Century* 85, 7 (February 14, 1968): 191–96. This article announced themes developed in her book *Faith and Fratricide: The Theological Roots of Antisemitism* (New York: Seabury Press, 1974).

5. On the connection between Christian triumphalism and Christian spiritualizing of the Jewish scriptures (and the identity and hope of Israel), see further John

T. Pawlikowski, "The Historicizing of the Eschatological: The Spiritualizing of the Eschatological: Some Reflections," in *Antisemitism and the Foundations of Christianity*, ed. Alan T. Davies (New York: Paulist Press, 1979), 151–66.

6. See Krister Stendahl, *Paul among Jews and Gentiles and Other Essays* (Philadelphia: Fortress Press, 1976), 132.

7. J. Christiaan Beker, *Paul's Apocalyptic Gospel: The Coming Triumph of God* (Philadelphia: Fortress Press, 1982).

8. *Paul's Apocalyptic Gospel* provides the hermeneutical sequel to Beker's acclaimed work *Paul the Apostle: The Triumph of God in Life and Thought*, 2d ed. (Philadelphia: Fortress Press, 1984), in which Beker puts forth his thesis that the core of Paul's gospel resides in Paul's apocalyptic hope of God's future transformation of creation.

9. Beker, *Paul's Apocalyptic Gospel*, 16. We must distinguish, Beker insists, between "the abiding or coherent elements of the gospel and its time-conditioned or contingent interpretations" (105).

10. "If Paul, for example, in his contingent situation does not draw the implications from his apocalyptic gospel that its coherent structure seems to warrant, we cannot simply repeat for ourselves the exegetical moves of Paul" (ibid., 105–6).

11. Ibid., 30–53.

12. I take this to be the import of what Beker says in *Paul's Apocalyptic Gospel*, 48–50. Beker "designate[s] the imminence motif in Paul as apocalyptic only in the sense that, with the [Jewish] apocalyptic authors, Paul expects the future to entail a definitive closure/completion-event in time and space, rather than simply a continuous, open-ended process" (50). Apparently, "imminence" as such is not one of Paul's central ideas.

13. Consider James D. G. Dunn's comments on 1 Cor. 15:23: "The metaphor [of the first fruit] denotes the beginning of the harvest, more or less the first swing of the sickle. No interval is envisaged between the first fruits and the rest of the harvest. With the first fruits dedicated the harvest proceeds. The application of this metaphor to the resurrection of Jesus and the gift of the Spirit expresses the belief that with these events the eschatological harvest has begun" (*Jesus and the Spirit: A Study of the Religious and Charismatic Experience of Jesus and the First Christians as Reflected in the New Testament* [Philadelphia: Westminster Press, 1975], 159). Bruce J. Malina has analyzed this and similar metaphors as expressions of what he calls "forthcoming" in ancient Mediterranean understanding and experience: "What is forthcoming is perceived in the same way as that which is actually present and to which the forthcoming is linked by an organic unity. . . . What is forthcoming stands at the concrete horizon of the present" ("Christ and Time: Swiss or Mediterranean?" *Catholic Biblical Quarterly* 51 [1989]: 16–17).

14. Beker, *Paul's Apocalyptic Gospel*, 104, 115–16.

15. Ibid., 82 (cf. 90, 118). Distinguishing his view from Bultmann's demythologizing program, Beker insists that the "literal" meaning of myth has a "double component." "It means not only a literal interpretation of its metaphorical im-

agery, but also a literal interpretation of its *real intent*—conveyed in and under its use of images" (82).

16. Ibid., 111.

17. Ibid.

18. Ibid., 110.

19. Ibid.

20. Ibid.

21. Ibid., 108. See also chap. 15 of *Paul the Apostle*, at the end of which Beker suggests, through a series of rhetorical questions, what looks like a similar set of hermeneutical moves (346–47).

22. Gregory Baum quotes John Pawlikowski's description of Christian liberation and political theologies as, in part, "a contemporary re-Judaisation of Christianity"—the "emergence," as Baum puts it "of an earthly and communal yearning for the fulfillment of the promises of God in history" (Gregory Baum, "The Holocaust and Political Theology," *Concilium* 175, 5 [1984]: 37). It is instructive to consider Beker's interpretation of Paul in the light of Pawlikowski's and Baum's observations. For Beker, it is Paul's continuing affirmation of Israel's history and messianic hope that keep his apocalyptic gospel anchored in history, thus preserving a significant continuity between the present order and the new creation.

23. Hal Lindsey, *The Late Great Planet Earth* (New York: Bantam Books, 1973).

24. E. F. Ströter, *Die Judenfrage und ihre göttliche Lösung nach Römer 11* (Kassel: Röttger, n.d. [ca. 1903]). The date of publication is uncertain. Ströter died in 1922. The book on Romans 11 must have been published between the time of Ströter's return to Germany in 1899 and the onset of the First World War, since there are references in the book to current events but no mention of the war. In an unpublished bibliography of Ströter's writings, Stephan Holthaus gives the publication date as 1903, but in his dissertation, Holthaus lists the book without a date ("Protestantischer Fundamentalismus in Deutschland—Seine Geschichte und Sein Erscheinungsbild (1800–1980)" [Louvain, 1992]).

25. In his opening remarks to the exegetical section of *Church Dogmatics*, vol. 2, part 2, sec. 34, 4, Karl Barth lists no other secondary bibliography for Romans 11 except Ströter's "extremely useful" study (*Church Dogmatics*, 4 vols., translated under the editorship of G. W. Bromiley and T. F. Torrance [Edinburgh: T. & T. Clark, 1936–69], vol. 2, part 2, 267).

26. Paul M. van Buren has recently acknowledged this debt to Barth, noting that while "what [Barth] wrote about the Jewish people horrifies many of us today," nevertheless "his radical break with the past cannot be denied." "Against the weight of the whole tradition, Barth insisted that the Jewish people today are Israel, as Jews themselves have always said. . . . For all his shortcomings, Barth taught us to say, 'the Church and Israel' and thus contributed importantly in ushering us into what may become the third great period of the Church's history, one that may come to be called that of *the Church with and for Israel*" ("The Church and Israel: Romans 9–11," *Princeton Seminary Bulletin*, supplementary issue, no. 1 [1990]: 7).

27. Aside from some differences in detail and argumentation, most of the insights found, for example, in Otfried Hofius's recent statement of the new view of the church and Israel in Romans are already present in Ströter's 1903 study. See Otfried Hofius, "Das Evangelium und Israel: Erwägungen zu Römer 9–11," *Zeitschrift für Theologie und Kirche* 83 (1986): 297–324. For a fuller treatment of the history of the "new view" of Israel in Paul, featuring a more detailed examination of Ströter's work, see Charles H. Cosgrove, "The Church *with and for* Israel: History of a Theological *Novum* before and after Barth," *Perspectives in Religious Studies* 22 (1995): 259–78.

28. I am not aware of any noninerrantist forms of Dispensationalism, but the Dispensationalist hermeneutic itself does not require an inerrantist position on biblical authority. A noninerrantist and therefore nonharmonizing "Dispensationalist" interpretation of the Christian canon is, in principle, an interesting hermeneutic possibility, although not one that I am prepared to advocate.

29. Ströter, *Die Judenfrage*, 8.

30. Ibid., 90.

31. Ibid., 52.

32. Ibid., 57, 194–96, 199–201.

33. Ströter regards the rise of Zionism as the beginning of God's historical work to restore Israel (ibid., 123–24) and envisions a day not far off when the Jewish people will make their home in Palestine. But given his criticism of militant Christianity, it is doubtful that he supported militant Zionism. When he speaks hopefully of what Zionism may accomplish, he imagines Jews finding a premillennial "homeland" in Palestine "under the Sultan or under some other worldly power," not establishing a Jewish state (126).

34. Ibid., 30–33, 76, 119, 177, 182, 199.

35. E. F. Ströter, *The Glory of the Body of Christ: An Opening Up of the Epistle to the Ephesians* (London: Morgan & Scott, 1911), 132–38.

36. It is a basic assumption of classic Dispensationalism that the millennium will be a time of national political life for Israel under the law. At this time Israel will fulfill its vocation to the nations, who will benefit from the light and justice of the law as it is extended to them as public law. Thus, in a prophecy conference address, Ströter applied Isa. 2:3 to the millennial mission of Israel among the nations: "Out of Zion shall go forth the law and the word of the Lord from Jerusalem" (E. F. Ströter, "Christ's Second Coming Premillennial," reprinted in *The Prophecy Conference Movement*, vol. 2: *Prophetic Studies*, ed. Dayton, 16; cf. Ströter, "Second Coming," 140.

37. Ströter, *Die Judenfrage*, 49.

38. Ibid., 102.

39. Ibid., 100.

40. Ibid., 100–101.

41. I draw this conclusion from the preceding. A further confirmation is Ströter's praise for modern Jews who keep the law (ibid., 90–91). By contrast, the

traditional Christian expectation of a final salvation of the Jews never led its adherents to affirm the continuance of Judaism because they did not think that the Jews, after Christ's death, remained God's people. It should be pointed out, however, that Ströter is thinking of the biblical law and not the dual Torah (written and oral) of the rabbis.

42. Wayne A. Meeks, "On Trusting an Unpredictable God: A Hermeneutical Meditation on Romans 9–11," in *Faith and History: Essays in Honor of Paul W. Meyer*, ed. John T. Carroll et al. (Atlanta: Scholars Press, 1990), 110–18.

43. Richard B. Hays, *Echoes of Scripture in the Letters of Paul* (New Haven, Conn.: Yale University Press, 1989), 35.

44. Ibid., 46. Recall the discussion of Hays's interpetation of Romans 9—11 in chapter 2, above.

45. Ibid., 45–46.

46. Ibid., 33.

47. This is the nomenclature of Greek rhetoric concerning disputes about legal texts. The Latin terminology is *ex scripto et sententia controversia*. See *Rhetorica ad Herennium* 1.11.19 (*[Cicero] ad C. Herennium*, trans. Harry Caplan [Loeb Classical Library; Cambridge, Mass.: Harvard University Press, 1954; London: William Heinemann, 1954], 34–35); cf. Quintilian, *Institutio Oratoria* 7.6.4–5 (*Institutio Oratoria of Quintilian*, trans. H. E. Butler [Loeb Classical Library; Cambridge, Mass.: Harvard University Press, 1921; London: William Heinemann, 1921], 3: 136–39).

48. Hans W. Frei, "The 'Literal Reading' of Biblical Narrative in the Christian Tradition: Does It Stretch or Will It Break?" in *The Bible and the Narrative Tradition*, ed. Frank McConnell (New York and Oxford: Oxford University Press, 1986), 36–77.

49. In theological discourse, *eschaton*, from the Greek term for "last," refers to the ultimate resolution of history in the new creation. Many of the earliest Christians, including Paul, thought that the powers of the new creation had already erupted in what they took to be the final moments of history, particularly in the resurrection of Jesus and the gift of the Spirit (see n. 13, above). Hence the story of the eschaton is the story of this eruption and its final consummation in the new creation.

50. Apocalyptic, too, can use a typologizing method to interpret the past. But it treats *itself* in a nontypologizing way as the absolute revelation by which the past, along with everything else, is to be interpreted.

51. See, for example, Richard B. Hays, *The Faith of Jesus Christ: An Investigation of the Narrative Substructure of Galatians 3:1–4:11* (Society of Biblical Literature Dissertation Series 56; Chico, Calif.: Scholars Press, 1983).

52. Norman R. Petersen, *Rediscovering Paul: Philemon and the Sociology of Paul's Narrative World* (Philadelphia: Fortress Press, 1985).

53. Hendrikus Boers, *The Justification of the Gentiles: Paul's Letters to the Galatians and the Romans* (Peabody, Mass.: Hendrickson Publishers, 1994).

54. Hays, *Faith of Jesus Christ*, 21–30.

55. See, for example, Jaroslav Pelikan, *The Christian Tradition: A History of the Development of Doctrine*, vol. 1: *The Emergence of the Catholic Tradition (100–600)* (Chicago: University of Chicago Press, 1971), 123–24. Bruce Malina has made a parallel argument in reconstructing what he takes to have been the likely attitudes of ancient peasant Christians ("Christ and Time").

56. Denis Farkasfalvy, "The Ecclesial Setting of Pseudepigraphy in Second Peter and Its Role in the Formation of the Canon," *Second Century* 5 (1985/86): 3–5.

57. In his meditation on Romans 9—11, Meeks stresses the unsurpassability of the literal sense, but in a way that also allows for typological or charismatic reappropriation of that letter: "We can hardly doubt that the Christ narrative (as Paul construed it) is unsurpassable—but in the same way that God's election and promises to Israel are 'irrevocable'" ("On Trusting an Unpredictable God," 123). Accordingly, Meeks proposes that, by a similar logic, "perhaps we can try to understand and to make fruitful for our present situation Paul's isolated and astonishing statement in 1 Cor. 15:24–28, which says quite explicitly that the time will come when the reign of Christ will be superseded and 'God will be all in all'" (123–24).

58. Walther Zimmerli, "Promise and Fulfillment," in *Essays on Old Testament Hermeneutics*, ed. Claus Westermann, trans. James Luther Mays (Richmond: John Knox Press, 1963), 106.

59. Ibid., 107. Cf. the following remarks by Ben F. Meyer: "In the dynamic tension of these traits [God's sovereign freedom and God's reliability], the factor of divine commitment somehow won out in the end over the factor of divine freedom. Still, the freedom factor made itself known in YHWH's surprising 'way' (*derek*). It was an ever-surprising way, flawless, facile, uncanny. . . ." ("Election-Historical Thinking in Romans 9–11, and Ourselves." *Ex Auditu* 4 [1988]: 3).

60. See Robert P. Carroll, *When Prophecy Failed: Reactions and Responses to Failure in the Old Testament Prophetic Traditions* (London: SCM Press, 1979). Carroll's focus is prophetic traditions reconstructed through modern historical methods. But his work is relevant to a study of prophecy as represented in the final shape of the canonical text, which ameliorates through reinterpretation but does not mask prophetic disconfirmation. For an example of a prophetic surprise, see Peter R. Ackroyd's observation that Isa. 29:1–4 prophesies a complete destruction, which was disconfirmed by an act of unexpected divine grace—a divine surprise that was nonetheless consistent with Isaiah's view of God ("The Vitality of the Word of God in the Old Testament," *Annual of the Swedish Theological Institute* 1 [1962]: 22n. 22). For a discussion of divine deception as a form of testing or judgment, see J. J. M. Roberts, "Can God Lie? Divine Deceit as a Theological Problem in Ancient Israelite Prophetic Literature," in *Congress Volume: Jerusalem 1986*, ed. J. A. Emerton (Leiden: E. J. Brill, 1988), 211–20.

61. Terence Cave, *Recognitions: A Study in Poetics* (Oxford: Clarendon Press, 1988). See also Christopher Prendergast, *The Order of Mimesis: Balzac, Stendahl, Nerval, Flaubert* (Cambridge: Cambridge University Press, 1986).

62. Cave, *Recognitions*, 489.

63. Ibid., 24.

64. Ibid.

65. Ibid., 496.

66. Ibid., 24.

67. Ibid., 489.

68. I allude to the concept of "a sense of an ending" as developed by Frank Kermode in his book by that name, *The Sense of an Ending: Studies in the Theory of Fiction* (London: Oxford University Press, 1967).

Chapter 4.
The Right to Be Israel

1. William Watkins, "Our Rights as Man," in *The Voice of Black America*, ed. Philip S. Foner (New York: Simon & Schuster, 1972), 135, 139.

2. See Monroe Fordham, *Major Themes in Northern Black Religious Thought, 1800–1860* (Hicksville, N.Y.: Exposition Press, 1975), 130–33.

3. Or "all those from Israel—these are not Israel" (John Piper, *The Justification of God: An Exegetical and Theological Study of Romans 9:1–23* [Grand Rapids: Baker Book House, 1983], 47–48).

4. Israel B is thus a kind of "remnant" as bearer of the hope of Israel as a whole. On this concept of the remnant, see Ronald E. Clements, "'A Remnant Chosen by Grace' (Romans 11:5): The Old Testament Background and Origin of the Remnant Concept," in *Pauline Studies: Essays Presented to Professor F. F. Bruce on His 70th Birthday*, ed. Donald A. Hagner and Murray J. Harris (Exeter: Paternoster Press, 1980), 106–21.

5. The formulation with ηὐχόμην can be taken as a prayer. See Richard B. Hays, *Echoes of Scripture in the Letters of Paul* (New Haven, Conn.: Yale University Press, 1989), 62.

6. William Campbell has made this point, arguing that Paul sees himself as a Jewish reformer who has no intention of breaking away from Judaism. See William S. Campbell, *Paul's Gospel in an Intercultural Context: Jew and Gentile in the Letter to the Romans* (Studies in the Intercultural History of Christianity 69; Frankfurt: Peter Lang, 1991), 143–48.

7. Jonathan Z. Smith, "Fences and Neighbors: Some Contours of Early Judaism," in *Imagining Religion: From Babylon to Jonestown*, Chicago Studies in the History of Judaism, ed. Jacob Neusner (Chicago: University of Chicago Press, 1982), 4.

8. On this subject, see Rosemary Radford Ruether, "Standing Up to State Theology: The Global Reach of Christian Zionism," *Sojourners* 19, 1 (1990): 30–32; Hassan Haddad and Donald Wagner, eds., *All in the Name of the Bible: Selected Essays on Israel, South Africa, and American Christian Fundamentalism* (Chicago: Palestinian Human Rights Campaign, 1985). For a broader discussion, see also Cornel

West, *Race Matters* (Boston: Beacon Press, 1993), 69–80; Michael Lerner and Cornel West, *Jews and Blacks: Let the Healing Begin* (New York: G. P. Putnam's Sons, 1995). I hasten to emphasize that my own focus here is the intolerance that springs from some forms of *Christian* political Zionism.

9. I am ready to endorse the symbolism of this phrase, "the church with and for Israel," which was coined by Paul van Buren (see Charles H. Cosgrove, "The Church *with and for* Israel: History of a Theological *Novum* before and after Barth," *Perspectives in Religious Studies* 22 [1995]: 263), as long as it does not suggest that Jews and Christians in solidarity are the political favorites of God (which, I hasten to add, van Buren does not by any means contend).

10. Studies of "nationalism," "ethnonationalism," and "tribalism" in the late twentieth century supply ample evidence of this. For a survey and penetrating discussion, see Tony Judt, "The New Old Nationalism," *New York Review of Books* 41, 10 (May 26, 1994): 44–51.

11. I am not contesting the claim that others have made important contributions to the Western human rights tradition. But certainly, there is truth in the case that has so often been made for a positive contribution of Pauline Christianity. See, for example, Ernst Troeltsch, *The Social Teachings of the Christian Churches*, trans. Olive Wyon, with an introduction by H. Richard Niebuhr (New York: Harper & Brothers, 1960), 1:82–86; Max Stackhouse, *Creeds, Society, and Human Rights: A Study in Three Cultures* (Grand Rapids: Wm. B. Eerdmans Publishing Co., 1984).

12. See further Elizabeth A. Castelli, *Imitating Paul: A Discourse of Power* (Literary Currents in Biblical Interpretation; Louisville, Ky.: Westminster/John Knox Press, 1991), on the way in which Paul's universalism is implicated with a tendency to suppress "difference" through an imperial value of sameness/unity. It is important to stress that in this respect Paul was a child of his time. Moreover, judged in comparison to typical expressions of the dominant ancient ideology of sameness that Castelli criticizes, Paul looks, at points, very tolerant and—from our perspective—progressive. This is not to minimize the importance of Castelli's study, especially in its significance for how Christians use Paul (and Pauline language) today.

13. For a very sensitive and insightful discussion of this point, see J. Louis Martyn's application of Gal. 3:28 to debates about the value of "diversity" in institutional appointments in "Galatians 3:28, Faculty Appointments and the Overcoming of Christological Amnesia," *Katallagete* 8, 1 (1982): 39–44.

14. Daniel Boyarin and Jonathan Boyarin, "Diaspora: Generation and the Ground of Jewish Identity," *Critical Inquiry* 19 (1993): 720.

15. This question is anachronistic (or "presentist") in cast, since it treats a concern emanating from the current conflicts over identity as if it were a question that Paul could have considered. But it is appropriate to inquire into the implications, for our current debates, of Paul's teaching about the relation between kinship identity and spiritual identity.

16. What Paul says in Rom. 9:1–3 depends on the unspoken assumption that it

is natural to feel special affection and loyalty, perhaps even fierce attachment, toward one's own family and people. Thus, Paul himself *affirms*, by his argumentative assumption, the legitimacy of such attachments, when he avows that he has them, in order to credit himself with his Jewish brothers and sisters.

17. C. H. Dodd, *The Epistle of Paul to the Romans* (London: Hodder & Stoughton, 1932), 184.

18. Ibid., 183.

19. While some commentators take this as a reference to God's "foreknowledge" in a more abstract sense, the clause in context is epexegetical, intensifying the sense of "his people." William Sanday and Arthur C. Headlam (*A Critical and Exegetical Commentary on the Epistle to the Romans*, 5th ed. [International Critical Commentary; Edinburgh: T. & T. Clark, 1902], 310) take the phrase in the more abstract, intellectual sense of divine foreknowledge, but they adduce parallels (with γινώσκειν, not προγινώσκειν) that seem to favor a different meaning, namely, the idea of a special intimacy: Amos 3:2; 1 Cor. 8:3; Gal. 4:9. The closest parallel in Paul occurs in Rom. 8:29, where the phrase "those whom he foreknew" is also an expression of special divine love and not simply abstract foreknowledge.

20. In a dialogue with Paul, Jacob Neusner describes how he has been enabled to see the Torah in a new light thanks to his conversation with Christianity: "From Christianity, I learn potentialities in the Torah that I might otherwise not have appreciated; in return I want to contribute to Christianity the possibility of the knowledge of God through the Torah." (*Children of the Flesh, Children of the Promise: A Rabbi Talks with Paul* [Cleveland: Pilgrim Press, 1995], xxiii).

21. See David H. Kelsey, *The Uses of Scripture in Recent Theology* (Philadelphia: Fortress Press, 1975), 125–55.

22. In the well-known terminology of I. A. Richards, the *tenor* of a metaphor is its subject matter (what is being redescribed), while the *vehicle* is the description or figure itself.

23. Daniel Boyarin, "'This We Know to Be Carnal Israel': Circumcision and the Erotic Life of God and Israel," *Critical Inquiry* 18 (1992): 491, 499. The substance of this article can now be found in Boyarin's stimulating book on Paul, *A Radical Jew: Paul and the Politics of Identity* (Berkeley: University of California Press, 1994).

24. Boyarin, "'This We Know,'" 491.

25. Cf. Boyarin and Boyarin: "Further evidence that this connection [of circumcision with Jewishness as a biological/genealogical status] has nothing to do with racism per se is the fact that one not Jewish can indeed adopt Jewish identity by taking on Jewish practices and through symbolic rebirth (and for men, physical marking) as a member of the Jewish people. . . . More revealingly, however, the convert's name is changed to 'ben Avraham' or 'bas Avraham', son or daughter of Avraham. The convert is adopted into the family and assigned a new 'genealogical' identity, but because Abraham is the first convert in Jewish tradition, converts are his descendants in that sense as well. There is thus a sense in which the convert

becomes the ideal type of Jew" ("Diaspora," 705). See also Neusner, *Children of the Flesh,* 5 6, 19.

26. I have borrowed this language from Robert W. Funk, *Parables and Presence: Forms of the New Testament Tradition* (Philadelphia: Fortress Press, 1982), 111–37.

27. Boyarin, "'This We Know,'" 483–97.

28. Jacob Neusner, "What Is Israel?" in *The Foundations of the Theology of Judaism: An Anthology,* ed. Jacob Neusner (Atlanta: Scholars Press, 1992), 3.

29. Ibid., 2–3. For a more extensive theological elucidation of this idea and its relation to a Jewish univeralism (as opposed to the view that Judaism is an ethnic and even nationalistic religion), see Neusner, *Children of the Flesh.*

30. Thus James LaGrand, "'Gentiles' in the New Revised Standard Version," *Biblical Research* 38 (1993): 44–54.

31. Martin Buber, *Two Types of Faith,* trans. Norman P. Goldhawk (London: Routledge & Kegan Paul, 1951), 172.

32. Ibid., 172–73.

33. Many ancient Jewish and Christian texts express some variation on the idea of the nations making a pilgrimmage to Zion. See the examples listed by James D. G. Dunn, *Romans 9—16* (Word Biblical Commentary 38B; Dallas: Word Books, 1988), 572.

34. Roger D. Aus, "Paul's Travel Plans to Spain and the 'Full Number of the Gentiles' of Rom. xi 25," *Novum Testamentum* 21 (1979): 232–62.

35. Robert Jewett, "Paul, Phoebe, and the Spanish Mission," in *The Social World of Formative Christianity and Judaism: Essays in Tribute to Howard Clark Kee,* ed. Jacob Neusner et al. (Philadelphia: Fortress Press, 1988), 142–61.

36. The "Scythian/Ethiopian" pairing was commonplace in Hellenistic ethnographic descriptions of the contrasts in humankind, as seen from a Mediterranean perspective. See Frank M. Snowden, *Blacks in Antiquity: Ethiopians in the Greco-Roman Experience* (Cambridge, Mass.: Harvard University Press, 1970), 169–77, 196–205.

37. Michael Fishbane, *Biblical Interpretation in Ancient Israel* (Oxford: Clarendon Press, 1985), 367.

38. Ibid., 367–68.

39. I mean to extend Richard Hays's use of this expression ("echo of scripture") by applying it to the canonical level of the text, where Romans and Isaiah stand in an intracanonical relationship of co-determination.

40. Stanley K. Stowers, *A Rereading of Romans: Justice, Jews, and Gentiles* (New Haven, Conn.: Yale University Press, 1994), 288. Stowers makes a strong case that the implied audience (the literary as opposed to the empirical audience) of the letter is made up of gentiles (21–31, 287–89), not a mixture of Jews and gentiles.

41. The context shows that the use of ἐγώ is emphatic.

42. I rely here on a distinction made by Hans Frei. Frei argues that the modern path of hermeneutics, with its special debt to modern historical understanding, led to a collapsing together of an important distinction between narrative meaning—

and in particular, the *way* in which the realistic narratives of the Bible mean—and the history to which biblical narratives ostensibly refer. A defining characteristic of realistic narrative is the "coincidence of the story's literal or realistic depiction with its meaning," which, in the history of modern biblical interpretation, was erroneously "taken to be the same thing as the claim that the depiction is an accurate report of actual historical facts." This "category error," Frei argues, meant that the available literary approaches to understanding realistic narratives were not taken up as ways of exploring the meaning of the biblical narratives. See Hans W. Frei, *The Identity of Jesus Christ: The Hermeneutical Bases of Dogmatic Theology* (Philadelphia: Fortress Press, 1975), xiv; see further idem, *The Eclipse of Biblical Narrative: A Study in Eighteenth and Nineteenth Century Hermeneutics* (New Haven, Conn.: Yale University Press, 1974).

43. See Charles H. Cosgrove, *The Cross and the Spirit: A Study in the Argument and Theology of Galatians* (Macon, Ga.: Mercer University Press, 1988), 129–30.

44. Richard H. Bell argues that 11:19 is part of an argument whose point is that "Israel will come to see that the Gentiles, regarded with contempt in Judaism, have a closer relationship with God" (*Provoked to Jealousy: The Origin and Purpose of the Jealousy Motif in Romans 9—11* [Tübingen: J. C. B. Mohr (Paul Siebeck), 1994] 113). *Contempt* is a strong word. It would be fairer to say that ancient Jewish ethnocentrism, like the ethnocentrism of other ancient (and modern) peoples, ran the gamut from a mild sense of superiority toward "others" to more virulent attitudes.

45. I do not mean to deny that some opponents of Paul may have been Jews who took an interest in the effect of the Pauline mission on Jewish adherence to the law. But I do not find evidence to suggest the existence of some sort of competition between a "non-Christian" Jewish mission to the gentiles and the Pauline mission to the gentiles.

46. Emmanuel Levinas, *Difficult Freedom: Essays on Judaism*, trans. Seán Hand (Baltimore: Johns Hopkins University Press, 1990), 22. I have modified Hand's translation in one respect. Hand follows the convention of capitalizing "other" in translating *autrui* (the personal other) in distinction from *autre*. So as not to leave the impression that Levinas is speaking about God, and not the human other, I have used the lowercase.

Appendix A.
The Concept of Plausibility

1. For example, in their widely used text on research methodology, Jacques Barzun and Henry F. Graff write, "The commandment about furnishing evidence that is decisive leads to a second fundamental rule: *truth rests not on possibility nor on plausibility but on probability*" (*The Modern Researcher*, 5th ed. [Fort Worth, Tex.: Harcourt Brace Jovanovich College Publishers, 1992], 166).

2. E. D. Hirsch, *Validity in Interpretation* (New Haven, Conn.: Yale University Press, 1967), 171–98.

3. *[Cicero] ad C. Herennium*, trans. Harry Caplan (Loeb Classical Library; Cambridge, Mass.: Harvard University Press, 1954; London: William Heinemann, 1954), 29.

Appendix B.
Unintended Meaning

1. E. D. Hirsch, *Validity in Interpretation* (New Haven, Conn.: Yale University Press, 1967), 234.

2. Ibid., 23. See further Hirsch's quotation from Martin Heidegger, who does defend this idea (248).

3. We can explain semantic effects produced by the slip of one word (the omission of a negative particle, the substitution of one name for another), but complex semantic effects that are both coherent and significant are much more difficult to account for.

4. Stephen Knapp and Walter Benn Michaels, "Against Theory," *Critical Inquiry* 8 (1982): 723–42; idem, "Against Theory 2: Hermeneutics and Deconstruction," *Critical Inquiry* 14 (1987): 49–68; idem, "The Impossibility of Intentionless Meaning," in *Intention and Interpretation*, ed. Gary Iseminger (Philadelphia: Temple University Press, 1988), 221–56.

5. Knapp and Michaels, "Against Theory," 727–29.

6. I find it difficult to determine whether Knapp and Michaels are seeking to make Hirsch's point that the verbal meaning of an actual author is the only real meaning a text may have, or whether they wish to make the softer point that, methodologically, we always treat the meaning of a text as an author's meaning (and must do so even in the case of accidental meaning). I think they intend to assert both points.

7. John Barton, *Oracles of God: Perceptions of Ancient Prophecy in Israel after the Exile* (Oxford: Oxford University Press, 1986), 145.

8. Brevard S. Childs, *Biblical Theology of the Old and New Testaments: Theological Reflection on the Christian Bible* (Minneapolis: Fortress Press, 1992), 75.

9. Gerald T. Sheppard, "The Book of Isaiah: Competing Structures according to a Late Modern Description of Its Shape and Scope," in *Society of Biblical Literature 1992 Seminar Papers*, ed. Eugene H. Lovering (Atlanta: Scholars Press, 1992), 565.

Appendix C. Hermeneutical Election
and the Shadow Side of the Canon

1. This is the central point of Norman Gottwald's critique of Childs's canonical approach. See Norman K. Gottwald, "Social Matrix and Canonical Shape," *Theology Today* 42 (1985): 317–20.

2. Brevard S. Childs, *The New Testament as Canon: An Introduction* (Philadelphia: Fortress Press, 1984), 51–52.

3. Gottwald, for example, contests Childs's suggestion that the canonical process was generalizing, tending to efface the marks of social and historical root-edness and particularity in the tradition. "As far as I can see," Gottwald objects, "*the canon* is very historically and socially moored, and *I as interpreter* am very histori-cally and socially moored, and *the God shown in Scripture* is very historically and so-cially moored" ("Social Matrix and Canonical Shape," 320). In the same context, Gottwald suggests that Childs "may here be confusing the capacity of widely sep-arated historical contexts to address and inform one another with a severance from historical moorings altogether" (320).

4. Frank Kermode, *The Classic: Literary Images of Permanence and Change* (New York: Viking Press, 1975).

5. Kermode's own study of the classic alludes tacitly to this by taking its point of departure from a consideration of T. S. Eliot's imperialistic and elitist notion of the classic (ibid., 15–45).

6. On this change and its prehistory, see Charles H. Cosgrove, "The Church *with and for* Israel: History of a Theological *Novum* before and after Barth," *Per-spectives in Religious Studies* 22 (1995): 259–78.

7. Lloyd Gaston, "Paul and the Torah," in *Antisemitism and the Foundations of Christianity*, ed. Alan T. Davies (New York: Paulist Press, 1979), 67.

8. Rosemary Radford Ruether, *Faith and Fratricide: The Theological Roots of Anti-Semitism* (New York: Seabury Press, 1974), 95–107.

Bibliography

Ackroyd, Peter R. "The Vitality of the Word of God in the Old Testament." *Annual of the Swedish Theological Institute* 1 (1962): 7–23.

Aus, Roger D. "Paul's Travel Plans to Spain and the 'Full Number of the Gentiles' of Rom. xi 25." *Novum Testamentum* 21 (1979): 232–62.

Bahti, Timothy. "Ambiguity and Indeterminacy: The Juncture." *Comparative Literature* 38 (1986): 209–23.

Barrett, C. K. *A Commentary on Paul's Epistle to the Romans.* Harper's New Testament Commentaries. New York: Harper & Brothers, 1957.

Barth, Karl. *Church Dogmatics.* Translated under the editorship of G. W. Bromiley and T. F. Torrance. 4 vols. Edinburgh: T. & T. Clark, 1936–69.

Barton, John. *Oracles of God: Perceptions of Ancient Prophecy in Israel after the Exile.* Oxford: Oxford University Press, 1986.

Barzun, Jacques, and Henry F. Graff. *The Modern Researcher.* 5th ed. Fort Worth, Tex.: Harcourt Brace Jovanovich College Publishers, 1992.

Bassler, Jouette M. "Divine Impartiality in Paul's Letter to the Romans." *Novum Testamentum* 26 (1984): 43–58.

———. *Divine Impartiality: Paul and a Theological Axiom.* Society of Biblical Literature Dissertation Series 59. Chico, Calif.: Scholars Press, 1982.

Baum, Gregory. "The Holocaust and Political Theology." *Concilium* 175, 5 (1984): 34–42.

Beker, J. Christiaan. *Paul's Apocalyptic Gospel: The Coming Triumph of God.* Philadelphia: Fortress Press, 1982.

———. *Paul the Apostle: The Triumph of God in Life and Thought.* 2d ed. Philadelphia: Fortress Press, 1984.

———. "Romans 9–11 in the Context of the Early Church." *Princeton Seminary Bulletin,* supplementary issue, no. 1 (1990): 40–55.

Bell, Richard H. *Provoked to Jealousy: The Origin and Purpose of the Jealousy Motif in Romans 9—11.* Tübingen: J. C. B. Mohr (Paul Siebeck), 1994.

Betti, Emilio. *Teoria generale della interpretazione.* Vol. 1. Milan: Giuffrè, 1955.

Boers, Hendrikus. *The Justification of the Gentiles: Paul's Letters to the Galatians and the Romans.* Peabody, Mass.: Hendrickson Publishers, 1994.

Boring, M. Eugene. "The Language of Universal Salvation in Paul." *Journal of Biblical Literature* 105 (1986): 269–92.

Boyarin, Daniel. *A Radical Jew: Paul and the Politics of Identity*. Berkeley: University of California Press, 1994.
———. " 'This We Know to Be Carnal Israel': Circumcision and the Erotic Life of God and Israel." *Critical Inquiry* 18 (1992): 474–505.
Boyarin, Daniel, and Jonathan Boyarin. "Diaspora: Generation and the Ground of Jewish Identity." *Critical Inquiry* 19 (1993): 693–725.
Brett, Mark G. *Biblical Criticism in Crisis? The Impact of the Canonical Approach on Old Testament Studies*. Cambridge: Cambridge University Press, 1991.
Buber, Martin. *Two Types of Faith*. Translated by Norman P. Goldhawk. London: Routledge & Kegan Paul, 1951.
Bultmann, Rudolf. "The Concept of Revelation in the New Testament." In *Existence and Faith: Shorter Writings of Rudolf Bultmann*, selected, translated, and introduced by Schubert M. Ogden, 58–91. Cleveland and New York: World Publishing Co., 1960.
———. "Is Exegesis without Presuppositions Possible?" In *Existence and Faith: Shorter Writings of Rudolf Bultmann*, selected, translated, and introduced by Schubert M. Ogden, 289–96. Cleveland and New York: World Publishing Co., 1960.
———. "Das Problem der Ethik bei Paulus." *Zeitschrift für die neutestamentliche Wissenschaft* 23 (1924): 123–40.
Campbell, William S. *Paul's Gospel in an Intercultural Context: Jew and Gentile in the Letter to the Romans*. Studies in the Intercultural History of Christianity 69. Frankfurt: Peter Lang, 1991.
Cardozo, Benjamin N. *The Nature of the Judicial Process*. New Haven, Conn.: Yale University Press, 1921.
Carroll, Robert P. *When Prophecy Failed: Reactions and Responses to Failure in the Old Testament Prophetic Traditions*. London: SCM Press, 1979.
Castelli, Elizabeth A. *Imitating Paul: A Discourse of Power*. Literary Currents in Biblical Interpretation. Louisville, Ky.: Westminster/John Knox Press, 1991.
Cave, Terence. *Recognitions: A Study in Poetics*. Oxford: Clarendon Press, 1988.
Childs, Brevard S. *Biblical Theology of the Old and New Testaments: Theological Reflection on the Christian Bible*. Minneapolis: Fortress Press, 1992.
———. *The New Testament as Canon: An Introduction*. Philadelphia: Fortress Press, 1984.
———. *The Old Testament as Scripture: An Introduction*. Philadelphia: Fortress Press, 1979.
———. "The *Sensus Literalis* of Scripture: An Ancient and Modern Problem." In *Beiträge zur Altestamentlichen Theologie: Festschrift für Walter Zimmerli*, edited by H. Donner, R. Hanhart, and R. Smend, 80–93. Göttingen: Vandenhoeck & Ruprecht, 1976.
Clements, Ronald E. " 'A Remnant Chosen by Grace' (Romans 11:5): The Old Testament Background and Origin of the Remnant Concept." In *Pauline Studies: Essays Presented to Professor F. F. Bruce on His 70th Birthday*, edited by

Donald A. Hagner and Murray J. Harris, 106–21. Exeter: Paternoster Press, 1980.

Coleridge, Samuel Taylor, *Biographia Literaria or Biographical Sketches of My Literary Life and Opinions.* Edited by John Calvin Metcalf. New York: Macmillan Co., 1926.

Collins, John J. *Between Athens and Jerusalem: Jewish Identity in the Hellenistic Diaspora.* New York: Crossroad, 1983.

Cosgrove, Charles H. "The Church *with and for* Israel: History of a Theological *Novum* before and after Barth." *Perspectives in Religious Studies* 22 (1995): 259–78.

———. *The Cross and the Spirit: A Study in the Argument and Theology of Galatians.* Macon, Ga.: Mercer University Press, 1988.

———. "The Justification of the Other: An Interpretation of Rom. 1:18–4:25." In *Society of Biblical Literature 1992 Seminar Papers.* Edited by Eugene H. Lovering. Atlanta: Scholars Press, 1992.

———. "Justin Martyr and the Emerging Christian Canon: Observations on the Purpose and Destination of the Dialogue with Trypho." *Vigiliae Christianae* 36 (1982): 209–32.

———. "Rhetorical Suspense in Romans: A Study in Polyvalence and Hermeneutical Election." *Journal of Biblical Literature* 115 (1996): 271–87.

———. "What If Some Have Not Believed? The Occasion and Thrust of Romans 3 1–8." *Zeitschrift für die neutestamentliche Wissenschaft* 78 (1987): 90–105.

Dahl, Nils Alstrup. "The Doctrine of Justification: Its Social Function and Implications." In *Studies in Paul: Theology for the Early Christian Mission.* Minneapolis: Augsburg Publishing House, 1977.

Dodd, C. H. *The Epistle of Paul to the Romans.* London: Hodder & Stoughton, 1932.

Donaldson, Terence L. "The Law That Hangs (Matthew 22:40): Rabbinic Formulation and Matthean Social World." *Catholic Biblical Quarterly* 57 (1995): 689–709.

Dunn, James D. G. *Jesus and the Spirit: A Study of the Religious and Charismatic Experience of Jesus and the First Christians as Reflected in the New Testament.* Philadelphia: Westminster Press, 1975.

———. "Once More, ΠΙΣΤΙΣ ΧΡΙΣΤΟΥ." In *Society of Biblical Literature 1991 Seminar Papers*, edited by Eugene H. Lovering, 30: 730–44. Atlanta: Scholars Press, 1991.

———. *Romans.* 2 vols. Word Biblical Commentary 38A and 38B. Dallas: Word Books, 1988.

Eagleton, Terry. *Literary Theory: An Introduction.* Minneapolis: University of Minnesota Press, 1983.

Eco, Umberto. *Interpretation and Overinterpretation.* With Richard Rorty, Jonathan Culler, and Christine Brooke-Rose. Edited by Stefan Collini. Cambridge: Cambridge University Press, 1992.

———. *The Limits of Interpretation.* Bloomington: Indiana University Press, 1990.

Evans, Donald. *The Logic of Self-Involvement.* New York: Herder & Herder, 1968.

Farkasfalvy, Denis. "The Ecclesial Setting of Pseudepigraphy in Second Peter and Its Role in the Formation of the Canon." *Second Century* 5 (1985/86): 3–29.

Farnsworth, E. Allan. *Contracts.* 2d ed. Boston: Little, Brown & Co., 1990.

Fishbane, Michael. *Biblical Interpretation in Ancient Israel.* Oxford: Clarendon Press, 1985.

Fordham, Monroe. *Major Themes in Northern Black Religious Thought, 1800–1860.* Hicksville, N.Y.: Exposition Press, 1975.

Fowl, Stephen E., and L. Gregory Jones. *Reading in Communion: Scripture and Ethics in Christian Life.* Grand Rapids: Wm. B. Eerdmans Publishing Co., 1991.

Frei, Hans W. *The Eclipse of Biblical Narrative: A Study in Eighteenth and Nineteenth Century Hermeneutics.* New Haven, Conn.: Yale University Press, 1974.

———. *The Identity of Jesus Christ: The Hermeneutical Bases of Dogmatic Theology.* Philadelphia: Fortress Press, 1975.

———. "The 'Literal Reading' of Biblical Narrative in the Christian Tradition: Does It Stretch or Will It Break?" In *The Bible and the Narrative Tradition*, edited by Frank McConnell, 36–77. New York and Oxford: Oxford University Press, 1986.

Funk, Robert W. *Parables and Presence: Forms of the New Testament Tradition.* Philadelphia: Fortress Press, 1982.

Gaston, Lloyd. "Paul and the Torah." In *Antisemitism and the Foundations of Christianity*, edited by Alan T. Davies, 48–71. New York: Paulist Press, 1979.

Gottwald, Norman K. "Social Matrix and Canonical Shape." *Theology Today* 42 (1985): 307–21.

Haddad, Hassan, and Donald Wagner, eds. *All in the Name of the Bible: Selected Essays on Israel, South Africa, and American Christian Fundamentalism.* Chicago: Palestinian Human Rights Campaign, 1985.

Hays, Richard B. *Echoes of Scripture in the Letters of Paul.* New Haven, Conn.: Yale University Press, 1989.

———. *The Faith of Jesus Christ: An Investigation of the Narrative Substructure of Galatians 3:1–4:11.* Society of Biblical Literature Dissertation Series 56. Chico, Calif.: Scholars Press, 1983.

———. "ΠΙΣΤΙΣ and Pauline Christology: What Is at Stake?" In *Society of Biblical Literature 1991 Seminar Papers*, edited by Eugene H. Lovering, 30: 714–29. Atlanta: Scholars Press, 1991.

Hirsch, E. D. *Validity in Interpretation.* New Haven, Conn.: Yale University Press, 1967.

Hofius, Otfried. "Das Evangelium und Israel: Erwägungen zu Römer 9–11." *Zeitschrift für Theologie und Kirche* 83 (1986): 297–324.

Holborn, Hajo. "The Science of History." In *History and the Humanities*, 81–97. Garden City, N.Y.: Doubleday & Co., 1972.

Hollander, John. *The Figure of the Echo: A Mode of Allusion in Milton and After.* Berkeley: University of California Press, 1981.

Holthaus, Stephan. "Protestantischer Fundamentalismus in Deutschland—Seine Geschichte und Sein Erscheinungsbild (1800–1980)." Louvain, 1992.

Jameson, Fredric. *The Political Unconscious: Narrative as a Socially Symbolic Act.* Ithaca, N.Y.: Cornell University Press, 1981.

Jeremias, Joachim. "Einige vorwiegende sprachliche Beobachtungen zu Röm xi, 25–36." In *Die Israelfrage nach Röm 9–11,* edited by Lorenzo De Lorenzi, 13–56. Rome: St. Paul vor den Mauern, 1977.

Jewett, Robert. "Paul, Phoebe, and the Spanish Mission." In *The Social World of Formative Christianity and Judaism: Essays in Tribute to Howard Clark Kee,* edited by Jacob Neusner, Ernest S. Frerichs, Peder Borgen, and Richard Horsley, 142–61. Philadelphia: Fortress Press, 1988.

Johnson, E. Elizabeth. *The Function of Apocalyptic and Wisdom Traditions in Romans 9—11.* Society of Biblical Literature Dissertation Series 109. Atlanta: Scholars Press, 1989.

———. "Romans 9–11: The Faithfulness and Impartiality of God." In *Pauline Theology,* vol. 3: *Romans.* Edited by David M. Hay and E. Elizabeth Johnson, 211–39. Minneapolis: Fortress Press, 1995.

Judt, Tony. "The New Old Nationalism." *New York Review of Books* 41, 10 (May 26, 1994): 44–51.

Käsemann, Ernst. *An die Römer.* 4th ed. Handbuch zum Neuen Testament 8a. Tübingen: J. C. B. Mohr (Paul Siebeck), 1980.

Kelsey, David H. *The Uses of Scripture in Recent Theology.* Philadelphia: Fortress Press, 1975.

Kermode, Frank. *The Classic: Literary Images of Permanence and Change.* New York: Viking Press, 1975.

———. *The Genesis of Secrecy: On the Interpretation of Narrative.* Cambridge, Mass.: Harvard University Press, 1979.

———. *The Sense of an Ending: Studies in the Theory of Fiction.* London: Oxford University Press, 1967.

Kincaid, James R. "Coherent Readers, Incoherent Texts." *Critical Inquiry* 3 (1976–77): 781–802.

Knapp, Steven, and Walter Benn Michaels. "Against Theory." *Critical Inquiry* 8 (1982): 723–42.

———. "Against Theory 2: Hermeneutics and Deconstruction." *Critical Inquiry* 14 (1987): 49–68.

———. "The Impossibility of Intentionless Meaning." In *Intention and Interpretation,* edited by Gary Iseminger, 221–56. Philadelphia: Temple University Press, 1988.

Kuhn, Thomas S. *The Copernican Revolution: Planetary Astronomy in the History of Western Thought.* Cambridge, Mass.: Harvard University Press, 1957.

Kümmel, Werner Georg. "Die Probleme von Römer 9–11 in der gegenwärtigen

Forschungslage." In *Die Israelfrage nach Röm 9–11.* Edited by Lorenzo De Lorenzi. Rome: St. Paul vor den Mauern, 1977.

Küng, Hans. *Infallible? An Unresolved Inquiry.* Exp. ed. New York: Continuum, 1994.

LaGrand, James. "'Gentiles' in the New Revised Standard Version." *Biblical Research* 38 (1993): 44–54.

Larrain, Jorge. *The Concept of Ideology.* Athens: University of Georgia Press, 1979.

Lausberg, Heinrich. *Handbuch der literarischen Rhetorik: Eine Grundlegung der Wissenschaft.* 2d ed. 2 vols. Munich: Max Hueber, 1960.

Lehman, David. *Signs of the Times: Deconstruction and the Fall of Paul de Man.* New York: Poseidon Press, 1991.

Lehmann, Paul. "¿Que está haciendo Dios en el mundo?" *Cuadernos teológicos* 10 (1961): 243–68.

Lerner, Michael, and Cornel West. *Jews and Blacks: Let the Healing Begin.* New York: G. P. Putnam's Sons, 1995.

Levinas, Emmanuel. *Difficult Freedom: Essays on Judaism.* Translated by Seán Hand. Baltimore: Johns Hopkins University Press, 1990.

Levinson, Jerrold. "Intention and Interpretation: A Last Look." In *Intention and Interpretation*, edited by Gary Iseminger, 221–56. Philadelphia: Temple University Press, 1992.

Lindsey, Hal. *The Late Great Planet Earth.* New York: Bantam Books, 1973.

Maier, Johann, and Kurt Schubert. *Die Qumran-Essener: Texte der Schriftrollen und Lebensbild der Germeinde.* Munich and Basel: Ernst Reinhardt Verlag, 1982.

Malina, Bruce J. "Christ and Time: Swiss or Mediterranean?" *Catholic Biblical Quarterly* 51 (1989): 1–31.

Martyn, J. Louis. "Galatians 3:28, Faculty Appointments and the Overcoming of Christological Amnesia." *Katallagete* 8, 1 (1982): 39–44.

Meeks, Wayne A. *The Moral World of the First Christians.* Philadelphia: Westminster Press, 1986.

———. "On Trusting an Unpredictable God: A Hermeneutical Meditation on Romans 9–11." In *Faith and History: Essays in Honor of Paul W. Meyer.* Edited by John T. Carroll, Charles H. Cosgrove, and E. Elizabeth Johnson. Atlanta: Scholars Press, 1990.

———. "Understanding Early Christian Ethics." *Journal of Biblical Literature* 105 (1986): 3–11.

Meyer, Ben F. "Election-Historical Thinking in Romans 9–11, and Ourselves." *Ex Auditu* 4 (1988): 1–7.

Meyer, Paul W. "Romans." In *Harper's Bible Commentary*, edited by James L. Mays, 1130–67. San Francisco: Harper & Row, 1988.

Neusner, Jacob. *Children of the Flesh, Children of the Promise: A Rabbi Talks with Paul.* Cleveland: Pilgrim Press, 1995.

———. "What Is Israel?" In *The Foundations of the Theology of Judaism: An Anthology*, Part 3: *Israel* edited by Jacob Neusner, 1–9. South Florida Studies in the History of Judaism 48. Atlanta: Scholars Press, 1992.

Niebuhr, Reinhold. "Martin Buber: 1878–1965." *Christianity and Crisis* 25 (July 12, 1965): 146–47.

Ogletree, Thomas W. *The Use of the Bible in Christian Ethics: A Constructive Essay.* Philadelphia: Fortress Press, 1983.

Pawlikowski, John T. "The Historicizing of the Eschatological: The Spiritualizing of the Eschatological: Some Reflections." In *Antisemitism and the Foundations of Christianity,* edited by Alan T. Davies, 151–66. New York: Paulist Press, 1979.

Pelikan, Jaroslav. *The Christian Tradition: A History of the Development of Doctrine.* Vol. 1: *The Emergence of the Catholic Tradition (100–600).* Chicago: University of Chicago Press, 1971.

Pelto, Pertti J. *Anthropological Research: The Structure of Inquiry.* New York: Harper & Row, 1970.

Perelman, Ch., and L. Olbrechts-Tyteca. *The New Rhetoric: A Treatise on Argumentation.* Translated by John Wilkinson and Purcell Weaver. Notre Dame, Ind.: University of Notre Dame Press, 1969.

Perkins, William. *A Commentary on Galatians.* The Pilgrim Classic Commentaries. Edited by Gerald T. Sheppard. New York: Pilgrim Press, 1989.

Petersen, Norman R. *Rediscovering Paul: Philemon and the Sociology of Paul's Narrative World.* Philadelphia: Fortress Press, 1985.

Piper, John. *The Justification of God: An Exegetical and Theological Study of Romans 9:1–23.* Grand Rapids: Baker Book House, 1983.

Ponsot, Hervé. "Et ainsi tout Israel sera sauvé: Rom., XI, 26a." *Revue biblique* 89 (1982): 406–17.

Posner, Richard A. *Overcoming Law.* Cambridge, Mass.: Harvard University Press, 1995.

Prendergast, Christopher. *The Order of Mimesis: Balzac, Stendahl, Nerval, Flaubert.* Cambridge: Cambridge University Press, 1986.

Räisänen, Heikki. "Paul, God, and Israel—Romans 9–11 in Recent Research." In *The Social World of Formative Christianity and Judaism: Essays in Tribute to Howard Clark Kee,* edited by Jacob Neusner, Ernest S. Frerichs, Peder Borgen, and Richard Horsley, 178–206. Philadelphia: Fortress Press, 1988.

Refoulé, François. "*. . . Et ainsi tout Israël sera sauvé*": Romains 11:25–32. Paris: Cerf, 1984.

Rendtorff, Rolf. *Canon and Theology: Overtures to an Old Testament Theology.* Translated and edited by Margaret Kohl. Minneapolis: Fortress Press, 1993.

———. "Canonical Interpretation: A New Approach to Biblical Texts." *Pro Ecclesia* 3 (1994): 141–51.

Roberts, J. J. M. "Can God Lie? Divine Deceit as a Theological Problem in Ancient Israelite Prophetic Literature." In *Congress Volume: Jerusalem 1986,* edited by J. A. Emerton, 211–20. Leiden: E. J. Brill, 1988.

Ruether, Rosemary Radford. *Faith and Fratricide: The Theological Roots of Antisemitism.* New York: Seabury Press, 1974.

————. "Standing Up to State Theology: The Global Reach of Christian Zionism." *Sojourners* 19, 1 (1990): 30–32.

————. "Theological Anti-Semitism in the New Testament." *Christian Century* 85, 7 (February 14, 1968): 191–96.

Sanday, William, and Arthur C. Headlam. *A Critical and Exegetical Commentary on the Epistle to the Romans.* 5th ed. International Critical Commentary. Edinburgh: T. & T. Clark, 1902.

Sanders, E. P. *Paul and Palestinian Judaism: A Comparison of Patterns of Religion.* Philadelphia: Fortress Press, 1977.

Sandys-Wunsch, John, and Laurence Eldridge. "J. P. Gabler and the Distinction between Biblical and Dogmatic Theology: Translation, Commentary, and Discussion of His Originality." *Scottish Journal of Theology* 33 (1980): 133–58.

Scalise, Charles J. *Hermeneutics as Theological Prolegomena: A Canonical Approach.* Macon, Ga.: Mercer University Press, 1994.

Schmidt, Karl Ludwig. *Die Judenfrage im Lichte der Kapitel 9–11 des Römerbriefes.* Theologische Studien 13. Zurich: Evangelischer-Verlag, 1943.

Schmithals, Walter. *Der Römerbrief: Ein Kommentar.* Gütersloh: Gütersloher Verlagshaus Gerd Mohn, 1988.

Schrage, Wolfgang. *The Ethics of the New Testament.* Translated by David E. Green. Philadelphia: Fortress Press, 1988.

Schreiner, Thomas R. "Paul and Perfect Obedience to the Law: An Evaluation of the View of E. P. Sanders." *Westminster Theological Journal* 47 (1985): 245–78.

Scroggs, Robin. "The New Testament and Ethics: How Do We Get from There to Here?" In *Perspectives on the New Testament: Essays in Honor of Frank Stagg,* 77–93, edited by Charles H. Talbert, Macon, Ga.: Mercer University Press, 1985.

Segal, Alan F. "Paul's Experience and Romans 9–11." *Princeton Seminary Bulletin,* supplementary issue, no. 1 (1990): 56–70.

————. *Paul the Convert: The Apostolate and Apostasy of Saul the Pharisee.* New Haven, Conn.: Yale University Press, 1990.

Segundo, Juan Luis. "The Hermeneutic Circle." In *Liberation of Theology,* translated by John Drury, 7–38. Maryknoll, N.Y.: Orbis Books, 1976.

————. "Ideologies and Faith." In *Liberation of Theology,* translated by John Drury, 97–124. Maryknoll, N.Y.: Orbis Books, 1976.

Sheppard, Gerald T. "Between Reformation and Modern Commentary: The Perception of the Scope of Biblical Books." In William Perkins, *A Commentary on Galatians,* edited by Gerald T. Sheppard, xlviii–lxxvii. The Pilgrim Classic Commentaries. New York: Pilgrim Press, 1989.

————. "The Book of Isaiah: Competing Structures according to a Late Modern Description of Its Shape and Scope." In *Society of Biblical Literature 1992 Seminar Papers,* edited by Eugene H. Lovering, 554–69. Atlanta: Scholars Press, 1992.

————. "Canonization: Hearing the Voice of the Same God through Historically Dissimilar Traditions." *Interpretation* 34 (1982): 21–33.

Smith, Jonathan Z. "Fences and Neighbors: Some Contours of Early Judaism." In *Imagining Religion: From Babylon to Jonestown*, 1–18. Chicago Studies in the History of Judaism. Edited by Jacob Neusner. Chicago: University of Chicago Press, 1982.

Snodgrass, Klyne R. "Justification by Grace—To the Doers: An Analysis of the Place of Romans 2 in the Theology of Paul." *New Testament Studies* 32 (1986): 72–93.

————. "Matthew's Understanding of the Law." *Interpretation* 46 (1992): 368–78.

Snowden, Frank M. *Blacks in Antiquity: Ethiopians in the Greco-Roman Experience.* Cambridge, Mass.: Harvard University Press, 1970.

Stackhouse, Max L. *Creeds, Society, and Human Rights: A Study in Three Cultures.* Grand Rapids: Wm. B. Eerdmans Publishing Co., 1984.

Stendahl, Krister. *Paul among Jews and Gentiles and Other Essays.* Philadelphia: Fortress Press, 1976.

Stöhr, Martin. "Learning Step by Step in the Jewish-Christian Dialogue." *Immanuel* 24/25 (1990): 267–79.

Stowers, Stanley K. *A Rereading of Romans: Justice, Jews, and Gentiles.* New Haven, Conn.: Yale University Press, 1994.

Ströter, E[rnst] F[erdinand]. "Christ's Second Coming Premillennial." Reprinted in *The Prophecy Conference Movement.* Vol. 2: *Prophetic Studies of the International Prophetic Conference, Chicago, November, 1886*, bound with *Addresses on the Second Coming of the Lord Delivered at the Prophetic Conference, Allegheny, Pa., December 3–6, 1895.* Edited by Donald W. Dayton. Fundamentalism in American Religion 1880–1950. New York: Garland, 1988.

————. *The Glory of the Body of Christ: An Opening Up of the Epistle to the Ephesians.* London: Morgan & Scott, 1911.

————. *Die Judenfrage und ihre göttliche Lösung nach Römer 11.* Kassel: Röttger, n.d. (ca. 1903).

————. "The Second Coming of Christ in Relation to Israel." Reprinted in *The Prophecy Conference Movement*, vol 2: *Addresses on the Second Coming of the Lord Delivered at the Prophetic Conference, Allegheny, Pa., December 3–6, 1895*, bound with *Prophetic Studies of the International Prophetic Conference, Chicago, November, 1886.* Edited by Donald W. Dayton. Fundamentalism in American Religion 1880–1950. New York: Garland, 1988.

Troeltsch, Ernst. *The Social Teachings of the Christian Churches.* Vol. 1. Translated by Olive Wyon, with an introduction by H. Richard Niebuhr. New York: Harper & Brothers, 1960.

van Buren, Paul M. "The Church and Israel: Romans 9–11." *Princeton Seminary Bulletin*, supplementary issue, no. 1 (1990): 5–18.

————. *A Theology of the Jewish Christian Reality.* Part 1: *Discerning the Way.* Part 2: *A Christian Theology of the People Israel.* Part 3: *Christ in Context.* San Francisco: Harper & Row, 1980–88.

Wall, Robert W. and Eugene E. Lemcio. *The New Testament as Canon: A Reader in*

Canonical Criticism. Journal for the Study of the New Testament Supplement Series 76. Sheffield: JSOT Press, 1992.

Watkins, William. "Our Rights as Men." In *The Voice of Black America,* edited by Philip S. Foner, 130–43. New York: Simon & Schuster, 1972.

West, Cornel. *Race Matters.* Boston: Beacon Press, 1993.

Winch, Peter. *The Idea of a Social Science and Its Relation to Philosophy.* London: Routledge & Kegan Paul, 1958.

Wood, Charles M. *The Formation of Christian Understanding: Theological Hermeneutics.* Valley Forge, Penn.: Trinity Press International, 1993.

Wright, N. T. *The Climax of the Covenant: Christ and the Law in Pauline Theology.* Edinburgh: T. & T. Clark, 1991; Minneapolis: Fortress Press, 1992.

Zimmerli, Walther. "Promise and Fulfillment." In *Essays on Old Testament Hermeneutics,* edited by Claus Westermann, translated by James Luther Mays, 89–122. Richmond: John Knox Press, 1963.

Index of References

Index of Modern Authors

Index of Subjects

co-deliberation. *See* rhetoric
coherence/incoherence, 22, 24
communicatio. See rhetoric: co-
    deliberation
covenant(s)
    Christian spiritualization of O.T.
        covenants, 52
    Davidic, 53
    God's, with Israel, 4–5, 7
    Mosaic, 53
co-determination. *See* interpretation
cultural-linguistic lexicon. *See* interpreta-
    tion

deconstruction, 39–40, 108
demythologizing, 48
Dispensationalism, 46–48, 52–55, 114

elect, the, 17, 69
elect community, 51
elect Judaism, 52
elect number, 9–11, 21, 34–35, 85, 87,
    103, 107. *See also* fullness
elect remnant, 1–2, 35. *See also* Israelism:
    elect remnant
elect, secret, 66
election, 1, 21, 27–28, 32, 65–90 passim,
    67, 89
    God's freedom in, 66
    irrevocable, 19–21, 32, 37, 74–75
    of Israel (*see* Israel)
    of nations, 84–85
    of "those from the law," 13
equality/egalitarianism, 49–50, 75, 89–90
Esau, 10, 28, 66–67, 72
eschatology/eschaton, 46–47, 49, 59–64,
    112, 115
ethnocentrism, 73–75, 121
ethnocultural identity, 76, 79, 84
ethnomethodology, 108
ethnonationalism, 118

faith, 12, 16, 37
flesh, social, 81. *See also* Israel, carnal
flesh, the, 81
fullness, full number (of elect, gentiles,
    Jews, etc.), 9–10, 15, 19–21, 32,
    34–35, 54, 83, 89

gentiles
    boasting of, over Jews, 87
    election of, 66
    full number of (*see* fullness)
    inclusion of, 86–89

the law and, 6
mission to, 121
as nations, 82
term as proper noun, 82
salvation of, 7, 21
God
    children of, 8
    divine deception, 63–64, 116
    divine hardening, 6 (*see also* Israel:
        hardening of)
    divine surprise, 63–64
    faithfulness of, 13–15, 24, 48, 78, 116
    freedom of, 10, 66–67, 69, 116
    gifts and call of (*see* irrevocable gifts
        and call)
    honor of, 6, 14
    impartiality of, 4–7, 9, 14, 16, 20–21,
        24, 29, 32, 37, 75–79, 84–86, 90,
        102, 105
    judgment of, 4–7, 14
    justice of, 27, 79
    love of, as passionate, 77
    love of, as irrevocable 79
    love of, for all human beings, 77, 90
    love of, for Israel/Jewish people, 8,
        76–78
    loyalty of, to Israel, 30
    makes political space for the gentiles,
        89
    mercy of, 7, 9, 14–16, 19
    passion of, 80 (*see also* love of)
    politics of, xiii, 86–89
    promises of (*see* promise[s])
    relation of, to history, 59
    righteousness of, 7, 14, 18
    "tricks" of, 31, 64
    trustworthiness of, 6, 31
    unpredictability of, 31
    vindication of, 48
    wrath of, 5, 12, 14, 27–28, 85–86

hardening, 16–17, 87. *See also* Israel; Jews
hermeneutic(s), xii–xiii, 120
    Dispensationalist, 114
    liberationist, 40, 108
    sacred, 37, 108
    special versus general, 38
    of suspicion, 4, 102
    of trust, 4
    of use, xiii
    See also interpretation
hermeneutical
    circle, 22, 38–39
    effect, 38

Israel *(continued)*
  blindness of, 16, 55
  canonical identity of, 26
  carnal Israel, 3–4, 15, 18, 20–21,
    29–30, 32, 35–38, 47, 51–52, 55, 58,
    62, 72, 74, 78–79, 81, 87, 99 (*see also*
    fleshly Israel)
  Christian devotion to Jewish people as,
    75
  as the church, 9–10, 22–23, 32, 95
  concept of, 90
  elect, xiii, 4, 20, 29, 32, 87
  election of, 1, 5–7, 10, 12, 19, 75, 78
  ethnic Israel, 1, 9–10, 20, 24, 30–1, 34,
    78
  ethnic particularity of, 79
  exclusion of, 12
  fleshly Israel, 3, 5–6, 9, 11, 27, 29, 53,
    66 (*see also* carnal Israel)
  genealogical Israel, 1, 20, 35
  hardening of, 1, 15–16, 19, 35, 54–55,
    69, 74, 86, 89
  identity and destiny of, xi, 4, 23–24,
    38–39, 51, 56, 65–90 passim, 69
  identity and vocation/calling of, 47,
    52, 55, 84, 114
  as the Jewish nation/people, xiii, 47,
    55, 69, 74, 78, 81, 95, 113
  literal Israel, xiii, 80–82
  meaning of, in Romans, 20, 95
  metaphorical Israel, 80–81
  nations and, 9
  national Israel, 29, 53
  the right to be Israel, 79, 90
  salvation of all Israel, 8, 13, 15, 19–20,
    29, 31, 34–35, 37, 54, 71, 74, 78, 83,
    89
  share in the age to come, 4, 8, 11, 18,
    79
  as sign, xii, 47, 51, 90
  as social metaphor, 81
  spiritual Israel, 1
  State of Israel, 75
  true Israel, xiii, 1, 4, 9–10, 17, 21, 24,
    32, 47–48, 52, 55, 65–90 passim,
    65–66, 69, 98, 103
  true Israelites, 5, 15
  twelve tribes, 66–67
  as type of the church, 51
  uses of name in Romans, 66–72
  vocation/mission of, 52–53, 84, 114
  as white America, 65
Israelism
  ecclesial, 1, 22–23, 69

  elect remnant, 1, 23, 69
  national, 6

Jacob, 10, 28, 66
Jesus Christ
  act of righteousness of, 19
  baptism into, 19
  canonical Jesus, xiii, 43, 72
  faith/belief in, 13, 15–18
  faith/faithfulness of, 17–19
  as messiah, 46
  resurrection of, 112
  as the truth of God, 19
Jewish
  apostates, 17
  exclusivism, 73
  nation, 2
  Jew and Greek, Jew and gentile, 1, 4,
    82
  the "Jewish sin," 74
Jews, Jewish people
  "advantage of," 5, 14, 21
  blindness of, 13
  "boasting" of, 18
  Christian Jews, 54
  Christian persecution of, 46
  as double signs in Christian canon, 74
  election of, 20, 37
  exclusion of, 86–89
  as God's elect, 11
  God's wrath toward, 32
  hardening of, 12, 20
  as heirs of Abraham, 12
  identity and destiny of, 4
  inclusion of, 33–34
  justification of, 55
  and law-keeping, 54, 114
  as negative foils in Christian interpre-
    tation, 73
  obligation to maintain Jewish identity,
    54
  as true Israel (*see* Israel)
  true Jews, 9, 17, 32, 73, 104
  vocation of, 53–54, 62 (*see also* Israel)
Judaism, 98–100
  associated with earthly, historical, 113
  as vocation, 54
kinship, 81
  identities, 76
  passions of, 118–19
  spiritual, 77

law (Mosaic), 1, 5–8, 53, 114
  adherents of, 12–13

Romans *(continued)*
  canonical Romans, xii, 26
  historical, xii
  imaginary ancient readers of, 2–3
  original meaning of, 92, 94
  original rhetorical situation of, 3
  as scripture, 41, 100
  as a text, 2, 102
rule of faith, 108

salvation
  dependent on obedience and faith, 13
  earthly, 47
  of gentiles *(see* gentiles)
  of Israel *(see* Israel)
  of whole creation, 48
  See also universalism
scripture(s)
  Jewish, 52
  literal sense of, 30
  plain sense of, 30–31
  purpose *(scopus)* of, xiii, 42–44, 72, 74,
    80, 90, 98, 110
  quotations of and allusions to scripture
    in Paul, 56
  resonances of in Rom. 9—11, 78
  use of the Bible as, 100
semantic effects *(see* interpretation)
social justice, 53. *See also* Paul: social
  ethics

Spirit, the, 5, 6, 9, 11, 19, 50, 59, 77,
  112
spiritual circumcision, 10–13
spiritual identity as ultimate, 76
spiritual kin, 77
spiritual sense, the, 58
supersession, 47, 87
surprise. *See* God: unpredictability of;
  rhetoric
symbol(s), symbolism. *See*
  interpretation
synagogue, 4, 6, 89

this-worldliness, 47, 51, 53–54, 76, 81
Torah, the, 53–55, 62, 64, 90. *See also* law
texts
  indeterminacy *(see* interpretation)
  nature of, as coherent/incoherent, 22,
    24
  uses of, distinguished, 41

universalism, 14, 19, 29, 48, 75, 77,
  79–80, 84, 118, 120
universalizing, 51–52
unsurpassable, unsurpassability, 48, 52,
  56, 59

vocation, 84, 90. *See also* Israel

Zionism, 53, 114, 118